30/4/94

P.O.H. Cartoon, *Peter the Great* by Colonel Hawker

PETER ORLANDO HUTCHINSON
OF SIDMOUTH, DEVON
1810-1897

Historian, Antiquary, Diarist and Artist

An Account of His Life and Times
Compiled from his
History of Sidmouth, his Diary, Sketches
and from Other Sources

For
Doctor Gerald Gibbens, *Curator of Sidmouth Museum, 1973-1986*

Whose help and encouragement
have made this work possible

Thanks also to my sisters
Margaret Anderson and Edith Whetham
of Cambridge

First published by the author 1983
Reprinted by Sidmouth Museum 1989
©Sidmouth Museum
ISBN 0 9512704 2 7

Contents

Introduction

Peter Orlando Hutchinson came to Sidmouth with his family in January 1825. He was then aged 15 and he lived in Sidmouth until his death in 1897, aged 87. His five volume manuscript *History of Sidmouth* has always been known, but the Diary and Sketches, though referred to in the History, were only located in 1980.* The five volumes of the Diary and six volumes of Sketches have brought a new chapter to Sidmouth's story: they give a vivid picture of 19th century social life, and the interests and occupations of the gentry. They were mostly professional, clerical and retired service families, who had moved in to enjoy the advantages of a prosperous watering place, one of many which had expanded round the coast when wars on the continent made foreign travel dangerous. In the Diary there are also glimpses of the true Sidmouthians, fisherfolk, farmers, agricultural workers, tradesmen and domestic servants, whose toil made possible an easy and carefree life for the Incomers. Some of the old Sidmouth names can be traced back to 13th century documents, when the manor was held by the abbey of St. Michael's Mount in Normandy. There exists a Cartulary, compiled by a monk in the dependent Priory at Otterton, which lists the names and holdings of Sidmouth tenants and the customs of the manor.

Little was known of Peter Hutchinson's early life, but now, thanks to the Diary and Sketches, it has been possible to piece together something of his childhood, youth and family history; an account can be given of his walking tours and travels, and of his visit to Canada, and to America where his Hutchinson ancestors had settled from Lincolnshire in the 17th century. His lifelong urge to write began in his youth and became almost an obsession. Much of his early work he destroyed, together with the first fifteen years of his Diary, except for a few extracts he retained; the main part of the Diary starts in 1848 and continues for forty-six years.

His elder brother, Young Bingham, and his sister Frances Harriet married and emigrated with early colonists to South Australia. His father died in 1846 and his mother in 1855. Peter then let the family home at 4 Coburg Terrace for a year, which he spent mostly in France before returning to enjoy a modest income, independence and leisure to follow his own interests. He began to collect data for his History of Sidmouth in about 1849, and continued researches for it until 1882; he then wrote that the third manuscript copy was at last finished and laid aside. Peter was active in the social and cultural life of the town and developed his many

*in Exeter Record Office & West Country Studies Library. Photo copies in Sidmouth Museum.

interests with enthusiasm. He was welcomed at most of the local houses for a variety of parties and outings; he also paid long visits to relatives in Chudleigh, Dawlish, Uffculme and Staffordshire. His return of hospitality was meagre; afternoon tea, he wrote, was a useful innovation, needing little preparation or expense.

The even tenor of Peter's life was only once seriously disrupted. In 1858 a committee was formed to consider the restoration of the parish church; Peter was a member; so much money was collected that the plan for improvements was discarded for an almost total rebuilding, except for the tower. Awesome controversy and dreadful quarrels ensued, in which Peter fought almost alone for moderation and preservation. He saved the medieval glass and some ancient stone carvings; he had the old chancel re-erected on his land to form the first part of the stone mansion known as The Old Chancel. He prevented the Queen's being involved over a memorial window to her father the Duke of Kent (who died in Sidmouth in 1820), with his epic visit to Osborne to petition his sovereign. His work on his house occupied much of his time and energy for the rest of his life; it has a gloomy semi-medieval appearance reflecting its creator's outlook. Perhaps it was his defence against life's troubles, and a refuge in his lonely old age.

Peter Orlando Hutchinson was a Sidmouth benefactor and notable, who deserves to be remembered and honoured. This account is intended to renew interest in his life and times: the History, Diary and Sketches are now available for study and it is hoped they may encourage others to record today's events for tomorrow's local historians.

Forebears and Family

Peter traced his Hutchinson ancestors back nine generations to Alford in Lincolnshire. In the 17th century Edward and Susanna Hutchinson emigrated to America. They had eight children, and it was from their eldest son William, that Peter was directly descended. American, English Irish and later Australian branches were founded and Peter made and distributed their pedigrees. His visit by sailing ship to America in 1837-1838 gave him an insight into their lives especially those of his great grandfather, Thomas Hutchinson, Governor of Massachusetts and his grandfather, Thomas II, a Probate Judge, both of whom had fled to England with other loyalists during the American Revolution. They lost almost all their possessions in and around Boston. Peter spent some time there; he visited and sketched his great grandfather's house in Boston. The American connection was certainly important in his life; it was renewed when he acquired Governor Hutchinson's papers on the death of a cousin. They were in a confused mass and took time to sort and study. Peter realised their historical interest and he eventually edited and published two volumes of his great grandfather's Diary and Letters in 1884 and 1886. It is a history of the American Revolution from the loyalist side, showing the plight and impoverishment of the Government supporters. It seems that Governor Hutchinson was three times offered a baronetcy by George III for his services; but refused because of his poverty. Peter set great store by such honours and titles and bemoaned his own lowly state. When he met distant cousins the Earl and Countess of Donoughmore—(descended from Richard, a younger son of Edward and Susanna Hutchinson), he wrote:- 'They are earls and I am nothing.'

In the last chapter of Volume II brief biographies and pedigrees of the Hutchinson family are given; they show the extent of Peter's interest in his ancestry.

Governor Hutchinson settled in Croydon; he died there in 1780 and was buried in the old church with three of his children. His great grandson had a memorial brass tablet placed in the new church on 3rd June 1885, exactly one hundred and five years after the Governor's death. The text from the Diary 3rd June 1885:-

THOMAS HUTCHINSON ESQ. B.A. (HARVARD) DCL. (OXON)
CAPTAIN GENERAL AND GOVERNOR IN CHIEF
OF THE LATE PROVINCE OF MASSACHUSETTS BAY
IN NORTH AMERICA
SON OF THOMAS H. AND SARA (FOSTER)
SON OF ELISHA H. AND HANNAH (HAWKINS)
SON OF EDWARD H. AND CATHERINE (HANBY)
SON OF WILLIAM H. AND ANNE (MARBURY)
SON OF EDWARD HUTCHINSON AND HIS WIFE SUSANNE
OF ALFORD IN THE COUNTY OF LINCOLN
HE WAS BORN SEPT. 9TH 1711 AND DIED JUNE 3RD 1780,
AND WAS INTERRED IN A VAULT UNDER THIS CHURCH

Governor Hutchinson's eldest son Thomas II married Sarah Oliver, daughter of Lieutenant Governor Andrew Oliver of Massachusetts. They fled from the Revolution in 1776 with their two elder children; Andrew, their third child and Peter's father, was born at sea, as they sailed for England to join the ranks of exiled loyalists. For financial and health reasons they lived in France for some years, enabling Andrew to learn the language which he later taught Peter. The family finally settled at Wonford House, Heavitree, then a village near Exeter.

His wife Sarah died in 1802 and Thomas in 1811; they were buried in Heavitree old church, so Peter never knew his Hutchinson grandparents.

Andrew went to Exeter Grammar School until in 1795 he was apprenticed to Mr. Samuel Luscombe a surgeon at the Devon and Exeter Hospital. In 1797 he went to Catherine Hall, Cambridge—now St. Catherine's College. From the college records it seems he entered as a sizar matriculated in the Lent term 1799 and obtained an M.B. degree in 1801. In January, of that year he was appointed Physician to the Hospital, where he served until his resignation in 1804. He became a Fellow of the Royal Society in that year. From the Society's records it seems he was elected by application sponsored by other Fellows.

No record has been found of any special work of research done to obtain this honour. His son Peter was clearly proud of it and had it engraved on his own memorial tablet in Sidmouth church and on his father's and his own gravestones.

Dr. Andrew Hutchinson married in 1805 Anne Parker, fifth daughter of Admiral Sir William Parker, whose exploits at sea, including the battle of St. Vincent in 1797 are mentioned in the Diary with pride. His mother's four sisters and their children provided Peter with many pleasant holidays. The Hutchinsons first lived at Richmond near the widowed Lady Parker, where their eldest son, Young Bingham, was born and where two daughters died in infancy. Peter was born on 17th November 1810 at Winchester, where Dr. Andrew was a hospital physician. They were not long in Winchester for their only surviving daughter Frances Harriet was born at Tiverton in 1812, also a son, William George, in 1813. They lived in a large house in St. Peter's Street, adjoining the churchyard with a garden running down to the river Exe. They had a brief period in Teignmouth in 1819-1820 perhaps for the children's health, for Peter was always delicate and William George died aged nine years.

There is only one reference in the Diary to Dr. Andrew's practice in Sidmouth. He attended Lady Prideaux of Netherton Hall, Farway; she had caught smallpox at the New London Inn in Exeter. The doctor kept two horses in the stables behind his house at 4 Coburg Terrace, so he must have ridden or driven out to visit the lady. Peter records she was a Miss Bernard of Cottington. She died, and there followed a legal wrangle by Sir Edmund Prideaux, who made a claim demanding her alleged reversion of money from her mother's estate. Sir Edmund married twice more and the Diary gives scandal and gossip concerning these ladies, adding:- 'Is the saying true that no man outlives his fourth wife?'(He didn't).

The Prideaux family had been lords of Sidmouth manor for six generations but the estate was bankrupt like so many others at that time, when their owners lived extravagantly off their rents without conserving and improving the land.

There are drawings in the Sketches of Peter's parents—a stolid looking doctor, his wife nursing a large cat; she looks kind and homely. There is also a self-portrait dated 1848 in romantic pose—perhaps Peter fancied himself as his good looking contemporary Mendelssohn. Under Dr. Andrew's picture in neat script is written,—'Aulae Divae Catherine Cantabridgensis,' in tribute to his University years.

Young Bingham, Peter's elder brother, was in the Royal Navy when the family came to Sidmouth, doubtless intended to follow in his Parker grandfather's footsteps. He left the service, however, to emigrate to South Australia with the first colonists. Andrew held a block of 134 acres of land bought for £100 which Peter inherited and later sold for £1,000. Bingham returned to England, married Augusta Kingdon of Narracot in 1852, and returned to Australia. He died in 1870, leaving a widow and four surviving children who were Peter's closest relatives; his sister Frances married Charles Rumley, the eldest son of General Rumley of Arcot House, Sidmouth. They too emigrated to South Australia, sponsored by Bingham and Peter with a £1,200 loan, There were no children of this marriage. Peter kept in touch with both families, sending out cots and clothing to his brother and side saddles and other necessities to his sister, as well as a share of their mother's belongings, silver and books, to both families.

Childhood and Youth

In a Diary entry on his birthday, 17th November 1881, there is a useful autobiographical account of Peter's life. He recalls his earliest memories of a carriage drive in Tiverton seated on his mother's lap and of his bouts of illness and pain in these early years which lasted into manhood; he had a left hip infection—probably tuberculous—and had to spend months in bed or on crutches. 'A poor little sick boy', he described himself aged about seven. Sea air, good food and prolonged rest were prescribed for this then prevalent disease. Memorials in all the local churches recording the early deaths of young people in the 19th century show how often the treatment failed in the pulmonary form of the disease, leaving sorrowing parents. Peter's early memories included his first view of the sea at Dawlish, of which he wrote—'I can see it now as if it were yesterday. There was a little ripple on the water from a gentle onshore wind, and the sea was of a dark blue colour. I could scarcely believe that all that could be water.' He also remembered seeing the Duke and Duchess of Kent in Teignmouth when they were in the South West househunting. They came to Woolbrook Glen (now Royal Glen) with their infant daughter Victoria, later Queen Victoria. The Royal Visit, however, was brief as the Duke died suddenly in January 1820. The party left with an astonishing display of mourning, in a doleful procession of black draped hearse, horses and carriages, through the town en route to Windsor.

Because of his poor health Peter was educated at home with tutors and at local schools. He studied and read French with his father, who, he wrote—'Had a good accent from his childhood years in France.' It seems Peter too had been abroad, or on coastal voyages. In his account of sailing home from New York in February 1838, he writes of having 'A good view of Dover—the Castle and Shakespeare Cliff. How often have I seen Dover this way, in a steamer, packets and various other craft—and yet never was there.' From his mother he must have learnt homecrafts for he wrote of needlework, embroidery and mending; in later years he always used a feather brush himself on his books, china and other valuables. His love of music started in Tiverton when a boy friend pulled a fife from his pocket and began to play. 'I was mad to learn music', he wrote, and so his years of musical appreciation and performance were founded in childhood. He played piano, flute and French horn, which enabled him to join in many music parties and concerts; he noted the hours he spent in practice in his Diary.

The Hutchinson family moved to 4 Coburg Terrace in Sidmouth in

January 1825. Dr. and Mrs. Hutchinson, Young Bingham (then in the Royal Navy) Peter, Frances Harriet, the cat and the canary. The house in Tiverton was sold to 'Mr. Heathcoat of the lace factory.' The Hutchinsons' new home was the end house of a charming Georgian row which remains much as it was over a hundred and fifty years ago. The house was owned by Sir John Kennaway of Escot; it was first leased and later bought with part of Blackmore field to form Peter Hutchinson's estate.

Sidmouth lower town had been devastated by the Great Storm of November 1824 which had ravaged the Channel coast; Sidmouth was still showing its damage the following year. This inundation is described in detail in the History, remembered from Peter's first view of the town and told by those who had endured it. There are glimpses of these early years and his boyhood interests; swimming in deep pools in the River Sid; ball games on the Fort Field with William, son of Mr. Wallis of the Library; an undiscovered prank with another boy, causing an explosion in one of the Fort guns; shooting birds in Woolbrook Glen; the companionship of C. F. Williams, son of Mr. Williams who had been a harpist at Powderham Castle before retiring to Sidmouth. The boys painted and sketched together, remaining life-long friends. C. F. Williams became a well known topographical engraver of the time. Peter visited him at Beer when he came on holiday from Southampton, with his latest batch of paintings and engravings. Peter's first encounter with an artist was when aged about ten; he was taken to see a crippled painter at work, holding his brush between 'the stumps of his arms.' This was Thomas Luny, the marine painter, who lost the use of his hands in later life.

Peter's interest in geology also began in childhood and was roused by a cousin who stayed with the family in Tiverton. 'My eyes were opened to the wonders of geology by a niece of my mother's,' he wrote, 'A very clever person indeed, who died a few years later.'

His interest in building was fostered by spending two years in an architect's office in Staffordshire.* He was probably living with a Hutchinson uncle or cousin, but the date and the architect's name are not revealed, only that it occured when he was a lad.

Perhaps it was his early experience of illness and his father's profession, which caused the morbid streak which is seen all through Peter's writing. Ghoulish details and drawing of human and animal deformities are given. There is a long account of the Siamese Twins he saw in America, and several entries concerning the appointment of a new hangman; death and disaster seemed to fascinate him; while in Paris in 1855-1856 he made several visits to the morgue before seeing the corpse of a drowned young man. It was a morbid trait, for while he declared such a spectacle should not be seen in public, he continued to go himself, even pushing through a large crowd of sightseers to gaze at the nearly naked body of a young woman, which he described in detail.

*in 'unspoken' speech by P.O.H. in Sidmouth Museum.

So the delicate boy, protected and cherished at home, a good classical scholar, earnest and studious developed into a young man eager to see the world beyond his family and near relatives. The long periods of bed rest and illness certainly affected his life; he had been often house-bound, isolated, introspective and dependent on home occupations and interests and perhaps cossetted by too many womenfolk. He still had bouts of illness which he thought were rheumatism and neuritis; he remained lame all his days, but he hoped to 'walk off' his infirmities. In 1833 he set out determined to be his own man and see the world.

Tours and Travels

In 1833 Peter Hutchinson began a series of walking tours, hoping to improve his health with a change of air and exercise. These early journeys can only be traced by the dated sketches he made; he had destroyed fifteen years of his Diary from this year, because he considered them childish and worthless. The sketches have survived, and very charming many of them are. In May 1833 he sketched Glastonbury Abbey, then Chepstow, Raglan, and Glamorgan; in June he was at Carmarthen and Pontypool; in July he saw Cader Idris and Snowdon followed by Conway Castle, Denbigh and Flint, on his way to Liverpool in August. Thence he took a train to Manchester, but of what must have been his first rail journey we have no account, though a lucky chance produced the information that he had been in Derbyshire and Staffordshire with an introduction to a pottery and a coal pit. Mr. Rodney Hampson of Keele, Newcastle, Staffordshire was on holiday in Sidmouth in June 1980, recognised the unusual name Peter Orlando Hutchinson in his obituary in the Transactions of the Devonshire Association, and recalled his partly quoted journal in an article in the North Staffordshire Field Club Transactions. He made enquiries at the Sidmouth Museum and sent a photocopy of the Staffordshire paper to the Curator.* Here, out of the blue, came part of a journal written by Peter aged twenty three. He had made his first rail trip, walked 1,237 miles, but there is only an account of his visits to the pottery and coal mine; they show careful observation and a determination to understand all he saw. His descent into the coal pit was an alarming experience; vividly he recalled the horror of the noise, dirt and darkness, for the mine was lit only by candles. He nearly collapsed and had to rest on a heap of coals; then he was taken to see Old Pluto the steam engine and furnace, in dreadful heat where, most shocking of all, were the men at work sweating, dirty and bare except for their trousers. The poor young man was glad to escape alive after an hour and a half! Perhaps this journal extract is part of the book he wrote after this tour but later destroyed.

From the Sketches other tours can be traced. He was in Shropshire in June 1834; at Haddon Hall, Buxton and in Staffordshire from June until September 1835, and at Hinckley, Leicestershire in 1836. In that year he also toured Scotland, visiting Culloden, the home of Macbeth, the Blasted Heath, and Forres and Spynie Castles, Elgin, Arbroath, Dunkeld, Edinburgh, Gretna Green, Ullswater and Liverpool. He was

*see Extracts pp. 40—44.

fascinated with the tales of runaway marriages he heard in Gretna Green and later he published *The Chronicles of Gretna Green* in two volumes.* Volume one deals with the place of Gretna Green in Scottish history and volume two gives the topography of the district and accounts of some famous runaway marriages. It ends with a chapter devoted to advising young women against elopement.

In 1837 Peter sailed for America and Canada. He stayed several months in and around Boston, Massachusetts and visited places where his ancestors had lived before the Revolution. He sailed home from New York in February 1838, the voyage taking a month. A short extract preserved from the destroyed Diary gives an account of his return voyage coming up the Thames to St. Catherine's Dock on March 1st 1838. In May, June and July of that year he travelled to Belgium, visited Ostend and Bruges. Perhaps he found it hard to settle down again with his parents, for in August and December he was again walking round Scotland, visiting Greenock, Glasgow, Dumbarton, Loch Lomond, Iona, Staffa, Inverness and Culloden. He also made a brief trip to Ireland in 1838 to see his godmother, Mrs. Jephson, and her son Sir Denham Jephson Noreys at Mallow Castle, County Cork. In June 1840 Peter was sketching Nunney Castle near Frome, also Cheddar and later Glastonbury. In February and March of 1841 he was in Hereford and Worcester, sketching at Goodrich Castle, the Wye Valley and the old bridge at Monmouth.

He travelled in East Anglia, walking much of the way in 1851, and went to Normandy researching for the records of St. Michael's Abbey and its Sidmouth holding in medieval times. After his mother's death in 1855, he again visited Normandy and spent some months in Paris. In 1857 he went to Lincolnshire to trace Hutchinson forebears. These journeys are fully documented in the Diary, as are his numerous visits to relatives in Chudleigh, Uffculme, Dawlish and Staffordshire, sharing their family life and exploring the neighbourhood. Peter was a great believer in a change of air, but it is possible there was also an economic factor involved. Sometimes he took lodgings in Exeter or Honiton and spent several weeks away, often taking with him his faithful delicate house-keeper, Ann Carslake Newton, who must have needed a holiday more than her master.

*there is a copy in the Cambridge University Library.

Life in Sidmouth

Mrs. Ann Hutchinson died in March 1855; her last illness is described with poignancy in the Diary. She was always subject to bilious attacks and her death certificate, signed by Dr. Miller, gave hepatitis as the cause of death. Peter, helped by the domestic, Eliza Lake, nursed her tenderly, coaxing her to eat, applying leeches and mustard poultices to try to relieve her pain; they sat with her in turns; all in vain, Peter had lost one of the very few people of whom he seemed fond.

After his mother's death, Peter let 4 Coburg Terrace for a year, most of which he spent in Paris, while the estate was being settled. Dr. Hutchinson had left him £500 and his land in South Australia; from his mother he had the house and £3,000, his share of the £11,000 she had inherited from her parents; this he invested in the Great Western Railway, 4% Preference Stock, With this modest income and a home he must have felt his first taste of security and financial independence. He settled back into Sidmouth life and took an active part in its social, civic and intellectual activities. He kept two domestic servants and maintained the standard of comfort to which he was used. One of his enthusiasms was for guns; in 1854 he was given a brass gun captured from pirates by his cousin, Lieutenant John Roberton in 1845; for this he had a limber built and, mounted on the gun carriage drawn by a horse, mule or local boys, he paraded round the town, visiting friends and firing his gun, or taking it on the beach for target practice, 'my appearance soon attracted attention,' he wrote in May 1854, after attending, uninvited, a parade of visiting Yeomanry on Peak Hill. Later he bought a new three pound gun from the Smethwick Foundry near Birmingham. It cost £3. 3/-, weighed 3 cwt., 2 qrs., 20 lbs., with a charge of 13/- for transport. The brass gun he gave to the Exeter Museum, in which he took a great interest, presenting it with many of his local finds and 'curiosities'.

For several years from 1859 he was a Lieutenant in the local Volunteer Corps, after refusing three invitations to join because of his lameness, and the expenses involved. However, he clearly enjoyed the uniform, the parades and the publicity.

Peter served on the Local Government Board and the Burial Board and the Church Restoration Committee. He joined the Archery Club and the Sidmouth Choral Society. In Exeter he became a member of the Devon and Exeter Institution in 1857, and the Architectural Society in 1860. In 1868 he joined the Devonshire Association and soon became active in its affairs as a Council Member. The Association was founded in 1862 by the geologist William Pengelly of Torquay, for 'the Advancement of Science, Literature and Art'; objectives which the members pursued with vigour, forming a pleasant club for the many well-read leisured gentlemen of the day. (There is a noticeable absence of any ladies!) In 1873 the annual meeting was held in Sidmouth, with the Right Honourable Stephen Cave, M.P. of Witheby as President. Peter was one of the Vice Presidents; others were—the Earl of Buckinghamshire of Richmond Lodge; the Reverend H. G. Clements Vicar of Sidmouth; Mr. W. R. Coleridge of Salston, Ottery; Mr. C. J. Cornish of Salcombe Regis; Sir J. Floyd of Powys; Sir John Kennaway of Escot; Lord S. G. Osborne of Cottington; Doctor Radford of Sidmount; and Mr. R. N. Thornton of Knowle. The Diary records the occasion in July 1873. The upper room of the Town Hall was converted into a museum; Broadway, 'the so-called Manor House' was opened for an exhibition of pictures; the annual dinner was taken at the London Hotel, followed by a soirée at the Vicarage. The final event of the meeting was 'a brilliant luncheon at Mr. Thornton's at Knowle';* Peter added;- 'Beautiful weather; some excursions were made.' In his address the first evening, the President paid tribute to the Reverend Richard Kirwan, Rector of Gittisham, a popular member who had drowned in Sidmouth while bathing the previous September. Peter read a paper entitled 'Submerged Forest and Mammoth Teeth at Sidmouth'. The severe storms of the winter 1872-73 had exposed these remains at the western end of the beach; they supported the tradition of encroachment by the sea all along the southern coast to the Scilly Isles, indicating changes in the level of both land and water over the centuries.

Peter was a busy man; his activities included many parties and frequent calls on his friends and neighbours. These, he wrote, 'took up much of my time and are a necessary part of social life.' He never married though he said he had always intended to. He loved the ladies, and his friends' little girls, pleasing them with kisses and sugar plums. It seemed that he felt marriage was a risky and expensive undertaking, but thought the alternative as a bachelor was also hazardous, leaving a man at the mercy of servants who were usually extravagant and dishonest. 'A necessary evil', he wrote of all except his housekeeper, Ann Carslake Newton, who served him for twenty-eight years (if she survived until his death in 1897). He left her an annuity of £28 per annum in his Will and counted her years of service in his Diary.

Among his many activities, Peter spent whole days on foot or by carriage in exploring the neighbourhood. A frequent companion was Mr. N. S. Heineken, a retired Unitarian Minister. With a pocketful of sandwiches, or a hamper of provisions and tools, they visited, measured, sketched and mapped the hillforts, earthworks, tumuli, churches and ancient monuments within a twenty mile radius. Long contented outings followed by discussions on these and other events, local political and the

*see Extracts p. 54.

scientific and cultural advances of the time; all are carefully recorded. He wrote too of the 'collections' made by himself and his friends, of paintings, etchings, china and curiosities of various kinds. Peter with his morbid interest in the unpleasant, stored away oddities such as a shark's jaw, a pig with eight legs, a kitten with two faces, Australian aboriginal skulls, a boa constrictor's skin, blood stained swords taken in the Indian Mutiny are mentioned; these he sometimes produced to startle and shock his guests.

Peter wrote of himself as a Jack of All Trades, and he certainly had many abilities which included handicraft skills, carpentry (which was done in the old stables of 4 Coburg Terrace), gardening, house repairs and improvements, needlework, book binding and the making of models were all part of his daily round. He constructed a summer house and with the help of three men it was raised into an elm tree. From its roof a flag staff was erected on which he hoisted flags suitable for the occasion. Royal birthdays, Waterloo Day and local weddings were so honoured. Later a forty-four foot flagstaff was erected in his field from which he flew even larger flags, including one of the Hutchinson heraldic arms, and a red ensign for the Prince of Wales' birthday.

Gleaning in the Diary, many references to Peter's health are found, which is not surprising after his early invalid years. He had two severe bouts of illness in adult life. In the winter of 1848-49 he had an inflammation of his knee, 'after a knock' and was laid up from November until May, unable to walk and having to hire a Delly or Delhi carriage to go visiting. He tried the application of leeches and blisters, and a change of air to lodgings in Exeter, but improvement was slow. Sea bathing he thought would strengthen him and in 1849 he records his almost daily bathes; but the fifty-first swim in October brought disaster, a severe attack of 'rheumatism' in his left leg, fever and pain which even the unusual treatment of a hot bath failed to reduce. Dr. Pullin was called and visited him again when he moved to Exeter lodgings. The doctor rode out from Sidmouth in time to share a nine o'clock breakfast. After these attacks Peter maintained good health for thirty years until old age began to discomfort him. He sometimes made Diary entries on his birthday; in 1881 he writes of his surprise at living so long and gives thanks 'to the Giver of all good things.'

In 1884 he was grateful for his good health and contemplates death with the calm resignation 'that belongs to every Christian Believer'. He still had thirteen years to live though he was troubled with bronchitis and began to fear the cold winds of winter. He spent more time at home, reading and writing in the library at The Old Chancel.

In a less hygienic age bugs were a constant annoyance and there are several references to changing lodgings because of them. After an encounter in July 1859 in an Exeter hotel he suggests a preventative; oil of lavender, applied to the edges of the nightcap to repel the invaders. Hot baths were a rarity but Peter was tough and took a daily cold sponge down, even when water in his bedroom was frozen, 'there is nothing to it, if done quickly,' he comments.

He mentions having his shroud made in 1883; his height as being five feet nine and a half inches; his long nose as being a Hutchinson trait. This however, came as a shock when the Reverend Lord Sidney Godolphin Osborne of Cottington showed him a profile medallion he had made. The entry is on 14th June 1873: he writes:-

'The Honourable the Lord S. G. Osborne invited me to go to the next room with him. There he uncovered a profile medallion of my own face and head, looking to the dexter side, about half size, which he had been modelling in clay at different times without my knowing. I confess I was considerably surprised . . . I did not know my nose was so long. My father had a large nose, and I presume some of my ancestors had. One of them, perhaps my great grandfather, the Governor, had been away on some official business, and was expected at Boston, Massachusetts on his return by water, on which occasion some American joker put the following lines in the paper:-

> 'When Hutchinson came, the people rose,
> to clear a place to land his nose.'

In spite of his local knowledge, Peter seldom gave lectures in Sidmouth; only four are mentioned. In January 1857 he spoke on Normandy and the Normans, in February 1858 on the antiquities of Sidmouth and neighbourhood and in January 1859 on Restoration of Churches.

In his old age in August, September and October of 1892 he gave a lecture, repeated twice, at The Old Chancel on geology, illustrated with drawings.

Peter was confirmed in Sidmouth Parish Church; he was a regular church goer wherever he was. In Sidmouth he sometimes attended three Sunday services and mentioned going to St. Giles in the morning, walking over the hill to Salcombe in the afternoon and then to All Saints for the evening service. In Paris in 1855-56 he went to a number of Roman Catholic church services, afterwards ranting about their 'popish practices', as he did against other 'wrong doings' such as those of profligate youth, drunkenness and the vices of fishermen after gains from good fish catches. He also disliked the custom of having to wear mourning scarves and hat bands, provided by the undertaker, at funerals to which he was frequently a mourner. This display was curtailed towards his later years, to his relief.

His home life at The Old Chancel seemed spartan. He writes of sharing cods' heads and hot cross buns with his much loved cat; he preferred an almost vegetarian diet, eating only one to one and a half pounds of meat weekly, and grew many of his own vegetables during his active life. The occasional gifts of a pheasant, partridge or hare from his affluent friends made a treat worthy of mention in his Diary. He changed his bedroom from front to back of the house each spring and autumn, noting the date, as he did for the beginning and ending of fires. Spring cleaning was also an important event, everything turned out, the Turkey carpet taken outside, slung on a rope between two trees and beaten, but 'never get all the dust out of it', he wrote. His china, pictures and books he looked after himself aided by a feather duster. 'Did you ever let the women put your room to rights, as they call it?' he asked.

In November 1868 after a lapse of several months in Diary keeping, he wrote he had considered burning it; 'What is the good, a diary which nobody may care to look at after I am dead. If I had a wife and children, I might wish to leave something after me, for their amusement or instruction, because men live in their children.' The seeds of his isolation are sown and there are several references to his single state. In December 1880, he deliberates again on matrimony; 'In spite of the bother and expenses and anxiety of wives and children, as I have heard married men say, it is better on the whole to marry and make the best of it. They then have somebody to live for and take an interest in, and they have somebody near them to hand their property over to without trouble. Had ladies not been such a costly people, I would never have remained as I am.'

It seemed a sadly gloomy philosophy for he could surely have used his talents to increase his income or have sought out one of Sidmouth's wealthy widows to share his life. Instead he maintained his isolation and perhaps had come to prefer his freedom from any family obligations.

The Diary entries are reminders that to the 19th century, the American Revolution and Napoleonic Wars were close memories but their anxieties seem also to foreshadow those of today, troubles in Europe and Ireland; war with Russia and fear of its power; the Indian Mutiny; and wars in Africa and Afghanistan, all have continued into the 20th century. Inflation too was a worry then as now. Coal which had come by sea at 26/- per ton was 44/- per ton; a labourer's wages had risen from 2/- to 3/- per day; a couple of fine fowls which Peter's mother could buy for 2/6 were now 5/- to 6/-. Rates and taxes increased each year though the value of property had declined. In 1888 he had to let 4 Coburg Terrace for £35 per annum whereas in 1879 he had obtained £40 per annum.

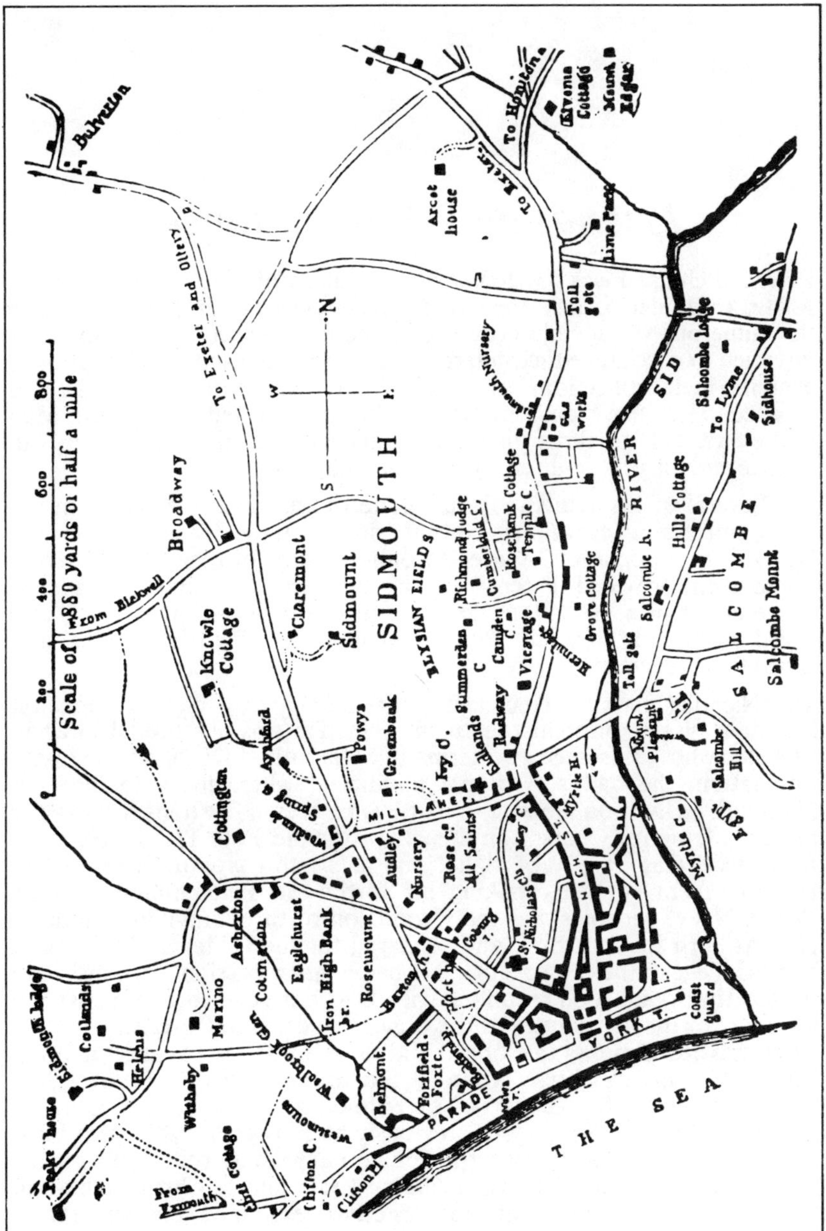

From The Sidmouth Directory, September 18th, 1869

Friends and Acquaintances

Peter Hutchinson was a welcome guest at many of the Sidmouth houses, for tea or dinner parties, for musical occasions or as an escort to amuse the numerous young ladies on picnics and other expeditions; sometimes he called to encourage their interest in geology, painting or carving, or to examine their 'collections' or invite them to inspect his own at The Old Chancel. He was certainly knowledgeable and enjoyed his rôle as a Man of Letters, able to share his interests and instruct his young friends in science and the arts while enjoying their company.

Several of his contemporaries stand out as close friends; from the Diary entries, and from their obituary notices in the Transactions of the Devonshire Association, a brief account of some of them can be given. These men provided Peter with the intellectual stimulus of shared interests, the pleasure of long conversations and discussions on local and world affairs as well as the companionship of their outings and expeditions together.

Mr. Nicholas Samuel Heineken (1800-1883) was a close companion for many years, until his death in 1883. He was a retired Unitarian Minister who had served two terms in Sidmouth, 1825-30 and 1835-40. The interim he had served in Cullompton where his wife died. In Sidmouth he lived on the west side of High Street, a few houses below the present Methodist Chapel, on the site of the old Poor House. He came from a German family of skilled musicians; his grandfather came to England from Bremen, making his fortune in Baltic timber for the British Navy. Nicholas was the second son of three surviving children. He was born in Yorkshire, and prepared for the Unitarian Ministry at York College in the city of York. He had a 'great passion' for music and studied the organ, soon becoming friends with the cathedral organist and a student of the mechanism of the organ. He came to Devonshire and in 1830 married Emma, the only child of Mr. M. L. Yeates, another Unitarian Minister, who served in the Sidmouth Chapel or Meeting 1821-25 following the first historian of Sidmouth, the Reverend Edmund Butcher of Helens. Yeates had previously been in partnership with Lord Rolle of Bicton, as a shipowner, trading in limestone from Babbacombe and elsewhere for local kilns, including those on the Chit headland in Sidmouth, abandoned about 1855. The business failed, but Mr. Yeates still had property in Budleigh Salterton, including a house known as Fairlynch, now the Museum. The Heinekens had one daughter, Emma, who married another Unitarian Minister, Mr. T. B. Floyd. Peter Hutchinson stayed with them at Wareham.

After retiring from the Ministry, Mr. Heineken spent the rest of his life with music, mechanics and the sciences. He had an organ in his drawing room and made his own double bass, taking instruction from Miss Leigh of Slade in Salcombe Regis. He played and sang in local concerts and attended music parties with the Exeter Oratorio Society. He invented a number of organ innovations as well as an instrument he called Seraphine, which was the precursor of the accordion and harmonium. He was a clever mechanic; he made his own telescope and lathe; the lathe is now in the Liverpool Polytechnic Museum. He was proud of his inventions and gave away his ideas without thought of any rights over them.

His many expeditions with Peter on foot or by carriage were a great pleasure to them both. The Diary gives detailed accounts of many such days, they would find shelter to rest and 'discuss our lunch' as Peter called it. They both joined the Devonshire Association in 1868 and Peter wrote a long and generous obituary for Heineken printed in the Transactions in 1884.

Dr. T. W. Radford (1810-1900) of Sidmount was another of Peter Hutchinson's special friends. They visited each other frequently. He was born in Exeter, the eldest son of Mr. Peter Radford, then house surgeon at the Devon and Exeter Hospital. Mr. Radford was godfather to Peter who must have been named after him (the reason for Orlando has not been traced). Thomas William Radford became a medical student under the celebrated Dr. Carpenter of Bristol, and later followed the still more celebrated Dr. James Martineau when he went to Dublin. Radford obtained B.A., M.B. and M.D. degrees but never practised, preferring to devote his life to science and literature as a perpetual student. He accumulated a vast store of knowledge, but was too modest and withdrawn to share it with others. He lived at Sidmount, with his brother George (who was a solicitor in Sidmouth), and his family. He was a generous supporter of all local charities—including the Cottage Hospital, the Dispensary and the Cricket Club. His speciality was the distribution of about 30,000 pairs of spectacles. Annoyed at the deception caused to the lace makers of the district by itinerant vendors of spectacles and the injury resulting, he began a campaign which lasted all his life and gave him an unusual fame in the South West. He seems to have had great charm and was a fine coversationalist, beloved by all who knew him. Certainly Peter found his company pleasant and stimulating; they were the same age, bachelors both, though the doctor was spared having to run his own home, a task Peter found arduous. Dr. Radford died in May 1900; Sidmount is now an hotel.

Henry Ede and family of Lansdowne, Elysian Fields, also gave Peter generous hospitality and friendship; they are often mentioned in the Diary. Mr. Ede seems to have been a cultured and kindly man. He had three children, and a pleasant home, he played the sax horn and joined in musical occasions and town affairs. 'My friend Henry Ede died this morning,' Peter wrote on 1st April 1887.

Another family who saw a lot of Peter was the Osbornes. They rented Cottington for several years in the 1870's. The Reverend Lord Sidney Godolphin Osborne of the *Times* was a keen amateur scientist. Peter kept him supplied with pond and ditch water for his microscopic studies. Picnics and expeditions were shared and Peter encouraged the Misses Osborne in their interests. At a musical party at Cottington the girls played two harmoniums, and one of the daughters helped to carve the stone bosses for the new pinnacles on the church tower in 1873: (recently removed as in a dangerous state). The Diary gives two pages of sketches showing the work in progress with the bearded Lord watching.

The family moved to Dorset after Lady Osborne's death in 1875. Peter clearly felt affection towards her and wrote that she reminded him of his mother; both ladies showing a 'uniform kindness'. Peter visited the family twice in 1876 in their new home on Poole Harbour; from here he explored the countryside and went sailing with his host; they visited Brownsea Island and attended church there. Lord Osborne died in Sussex in 1889: the event is recorded in the Diary without comment. An east window in the cemetery chapel in Sidmouth was dedicated to him in 1878 during his life.

The Reverend Richard Kirwan, Rector of Gittisham, was of Irish extraction; a genial and popular man of wide interests, which he shared with Peter Hutchinson and other Sidmouth friends. Kirwan wrote and lectured on many subjects; amongst them:- 'The Blights of Corn,' 'The Origin and Appropriation of Stonehenge,' 'Meteors,' and in the year of his death he contributed a paper to the Devonshire Association, meeting in Exeter, on 'The Aurora Borealis of February 4th 1872'. He joined the Devonshire Association in 1866 and soon became a useful member; he acted as local secretary for the Honiton meeting in 1868; he had obtained permission from the landowner to excavate the barrows on Farway Down; to entertain the Association members he arranged to open three barrows. Perhaps he found it a form of recreation, but helped by unskilled workmen he destroyed a great many barrows—digging for treasure rather than to gain knowledge of the people who built them. For his work on Farway Down he obtained a fellowship of the Society of Antiquaries. Peter commented on his excess of enthusiasm in the Diary, although he was guilty of the same zeal at times in the name of Archaeology.

Richard Kirwan was drowned in Sidmouth on 2nd September 1872. He drove over from Gittisham, left his carriage at the London Hotel, and walked west along the beach to bathe alone. Later his clothes were found, but he was missing. Peter wrote of hearing the news at The Old Chancel; of the efforts of fishermen to find the body, casting out a long mackerel net in a semi-circle from the shore in rough seas. Peter drew a sketch of the drama in the Diary. The body was thrown up later, severely bruised and scatched. Peter consented to be one of the Inquest jury, 'as I wanted to know the circumstances of the case.'

Among other friends Peter mentioned Doctor Benjamin Terry Hodge, M.R.C.S. and Licentiate of The Royal College of Physicians; he was third in a line of medical practioners in Sidmouth; he was devoted to his profession and its study, performing difficult and dangerous operations. He was also a keen sportsman with the rod and gun. Twice married he left one daughter; he died in 1883, the same year as Mr. Heineken.

Peter Hutchinson became an authority on local affairs and his advice was asked on many subjects. In June 1887 he mentioned being visited by Miss Maria Gibbons of East Budleigh and Budleigh Salterton (1842-1900), 'who has been touring Dartmoor and other places in a small carriage drawn by two donkeys.' She asked him to 'look over' proofs of her writing concerning the Sidmouth area. This redoubtable lady was the subject of a B.B.C. programme in June 1949. She is described as 'a stout middle-aged grotesquely dowdy lady, driving two donkeys tandem . . . sometimes taken for a witch or ogress.' Maria Gibbons published a number of minor works on her travels and also some verse; she is best remembered for the three 'Donkey' books about her journeys in the South West. She came to Sidmouth with a friend and wrote of her visit to Peter Hutchinson at The Old Chancel in *We Donkeys on the coast of Devon.* *

---

*see also Extracts p. 57.

Church Restoration

A very sad episode in the History of Sidmouth and the Diary was the restoration of the Parish Church which began with Victorian enthusiasm but developed into divisions, rows and most unchristian rancour in the town. The first mention of this affair in the Diary is on 19th November 1858 when Peter called at the Vicarage to give the Vicar, Mr. Hamilton, £5 towards the restoration of the Parish Church, 'soon to be begun, with an intimation that more would be forthcoming before the work is completed.' Peter looked at the old church with renewed interest and found 'a piece of stone built into the south wall of the chancel outside, having a Norman zig-zag moulding on it. This is a remnant of an older church at Sidmouth'.

A vestry meeting was called on 17th December 1858 to consider the plans, presided over by the Vicar. A committee was formed and there was discussion on reseating the body of the church. The members were:-

The Rev. H. F. Hamilton
The Rev. G. E. Deacon, Curate
Mr. J. B. Lousada of Peak House
Mr. Webber, confectioner of Fore Street (Church Warden)
Mr. W. Prittijohn, Ironmonger of Fore Street (Church Warden)
Peter Orlando Hutchinson

A faculty for the work was obtained in April 1859 and subscription lists were opened. So much money was promised that it was decided, after many meetings and much argument, to rebuild, leaving only the old tower and the nave arches, thus avoiding the necessity of a re-dedication; Peter was dismayed at this wholesale destruction of the old church and its ancient features;- two hagioscopes and the fine east window with its pre-reformation glass, with stone carved fragments from two earlier churches found during demolition, were to be discarded. He kept a detailed record and wrote *Restoration of Sidmouth Parish Church*, to which he referred those interested. It tells also of the Bone Business when the level of the churchyard was lowered by several feet, and the bones of past generations were found on local fields where the earth had been deposited. There was also a scheme to mutilate the church monuments (which had been removed before demolition) to make them smaller and easier to re-erect. Peter fought successfully to prevent this.

Many meetings were held at the Vicarage, in the vestry and Town Hall in an atmosphere of increasing animosity and vituperation:- those wanting a fine new church versus the preservationists: it developed into the High Church protagonists against the No Popery faction, until the town was seething with controversy. These dreadful quarrels caused Peter to compose an account of the whole sordid affair—an unspoken outspoken speech he wanted to deliver to his fellow committee members and to the town—but he did not. In this speech he wrote:- 'as regards myself, I felt I did know a little about church building, for when I was a lad, living near a personal friend, an Architect, who was erecting churches for a clerical relation of mine, I assisted him for two years in his architectural operations, making it an amusement, and receiving no remuneration. The insight which his practice gave me into the study of architecture was rather unfortunate as regarded yourselves for it enabled me soon to discover who knew something about it, and who knew nothing.' One hopes this long tirade relieved his feelings for he certainly had been deeply hurt and sorrowed by the affair. The culmination was the outrage concerning the placement of the Queen's window in the new church; this she had been asked to contribute as a memorial to her father, the Duke of Kent, who died in Sidmouth in 1820. It was solicited by one faction to embarrass and annoy the other, for the Queen was not told that the plan involved placing her window at the west end where the newly installed organ would block it; the organ, therefore, would have to be moved towards the altar, which the traditionalists considered to be a step towards Popery. Peter was filled with righteous indignation and patriotism and decided on drastic action to prevent Queen Victoria becoming embroiled. Backed only by the Earl of Buckinghamshire of Richmond Lodge (now Sidholme), who was a munificent contributor to the new church, Peter took a petition to his sovereign. On 19th September 1860 he went by coach to Honiton and on by train to Southampton and crossed to the Isle of Wight. In the dress uniform of the Volunteer Artillery, and carrying his sword, he walked to Osborne. He did not see the Queen but was asked to call the following morning when he was assured his petition would be considered. This was surely his bravest deed, for he must have known the consequence would be further verbal and written attacks on his opinions and actions. It was one of the highlights of his peaceful life. He describes the journey in detail in the History and Diary, and the storm of rage and abuse which enveloped him on his return for daring to act without the committee's consent. After several years when the feuding had died down, the Queen's window was erected at the west end of the church.* Thanks to Peter's efforts, the pre-reformation glass from the east window, representing the five wounds of Christ, was put in the vestry window of the new church; a lowly position for such a treasure, but perhaps safe from any modernising faction.

The main part of the rebuilding was finished in about a year, and the congregation returned in 12th July 1860. Services had been held in All

---

*see also Extracts p. 50.

Saints Church, segregated from its own flock by separate service times. The re-opening service was a great occasion, but Peter chose to play a schoolboy joke. He wrote in his Diary that he placed a paper the size of a £10 note in the collection box containing only three Bible Texts:-

1) Except the Lord build the house they labour in vain that build it. Ps. 127
2) It is an honour for man to cease from strife. Prov. 20, 3
3) And a house divided against itself shall not stand. Matt. 12. 25.

In spite of all the ill-feeling, Peter Hutchinson maintained his interest in the Parish Church: he did work on it, carving some of the stone capitals and impressing patterns on the walls of the aisles. He remained sceptical of innovation. Gas pipes had been fitted and the new lighting was used at Easter 1876. 'There was a great glare certainly' he reported.

From his wish to preserve something of the old church, Peter arranged to buy the old chancel. Unchallenged he signed a contract with Noah Miller the builder in September 1859 to re-erect the chancel on his own land at a cost of £45. Peter had discovered a creative and absorbing interest in building the Old Chancel house, an interest which continued for the rest of his life.

The Old Chancel

The foundation stone was laid on 13th October 1859, and the old chancel of the parish church was rebuilt, a little narrower and shorter. By 24th of November the eastern end with its window was completed and embellished with a cross, 'and looks very well', Peter noted. On 3rd December gables and gable ends were erected, also the chimney, crowned with a spare cross. On 15th December he reported the roof rafters being placed, but the weather was so cold that the men left, even after hot cider with ginger and nutmeg had been served to them. However, by 30th December the roof was finished and the floor 'earth-baked' preparatory to laying flag-stones. So began Peter Hutchinson's house building saga; the work continued for more than thirty years, and its progress can be traced in his Diary. On 4th October 1869 the Diary gives a résumé of the work done.

'In 1859 and 1860 The Old Chancel proper was erected on my ground out of the materials of the old chancel of the Parish Church, when the church was rebuilt: in 1864 I built the Oak Room on the north side of it with connecting walls, the window being part of the South Transept window of Awliscombe Church near Honiton, soon after carving the mantel shelf and brackets in oak, the bookcase behind the door, the cornice over the window, the painting, carving and gilding of the Gothic Heraldic ceiling, containing the coats of arms of the Lords and Lessees of The Manor of Sidmouth; and now I am going to make the place habitable by adding an entrance hall, with some lower and upper rooms, though not to complete the whole design.'

He punched this with steel letters on a piece of sheet lead measuring about six inches by four, and put it behind the top stone of the left hand buttress, going into the entrance hall. 'I am now engaged in carving the corbels in the four corners of the hall, from which the vaulted ceiling springs and the four corbels of the small vaulted ceiling of the short passage inside the hall. It has occupied me a great deal.'

Lime needed for the building was brought from the Budleigh Salterton kilns; those in Sidmouth on the Chit headland had not been used since about 1855; the remains of these kilns and the steep track leading to them from the beach, where the limestone had been unloaded, had fallen into the sea by 1871.

Much of the interior decoration and carving Peter did himself, and progress was detailed in the Diary. One of his first tasks was to lay some

Roman tesserae in the centre of the floor. They came from the Roman villa at Uplyme, which had been partially excavated in 1850. He bought 'a peck of them' in a sale at Musbury Vicarage in 1858 after the death of the Vicar.

In spite of the continuing work on The Old Chancel, Peter and his housekeeper, Mrs. Webber, moved in on 31st October 1866 and 4 Coburg Terrace was again let. The cramped conditions, dust and noise can be imagined: Mrs. Webber survived the strain only until January 1867. After serving her master's evening dinner on 21st January she retired to bed, complaining of feeling feeble and short of breath. Peter fetched her sister, Mrs. Mitchel, but Mrs. Webber died the following day.

In February 1869 a well was dug in the field behind the house to a depth of fifteen feet. Peter observed the strata and gave the cost of the work per foot. This year saw the start of the third building period when foundations were laid on 14th March for the entrance hall, two other rooms and a bedroom over the hall. On 6th January 1870, Mr. Ellis of Land (or Landpart) installed gas pipes. Between February and May stone bosses were carved for the arched ceiling between hall and staircase. On 13th April, four large gothic chimney tops were put up—made of terra cotta from Stamford in Lincolnshire; on 23rd April, William Newman, mason, fixed marble skirting in the hall. On 6th June the stone arched ceiling of the hall was keyed in and on 13th Peter estimated eight tons of stone had been used for it; he confessed to anxiety about his adventurous experiment as an amateur.

In January 1872 he reported entertaining a few friends to inspect progress, 'though my building is very incomplete'. In September he ornamented the doorway of the Oak Room with gilded diaper work. In February 1873 his fears over the chimneys were realised when the Oak Room chimney was blown down in a storm.

In January 1874 a suggestion was made by Mr. Sutherland, the manor estate agent that he should sell his estate so that a road could be made from All Saints to the Parish Church. Peter refused. In May he was visited by three of Lady Osborne's maid-servants from Cottington. He showed them the house and his curiosities and took them on to the roof to see the view. The same month repairs had to be made to the roof and the halliard replaced on the flag staff. Further repairs were also necessary in October and December 1886.

In February 1875 stone caps and granite balls were placed on the columns at the entrance from Blackmore Lane; the balls had been given to him about 1860 by the Earl of Buckinghamshire.

So year by year it is possible to trace Peter Hutchinson's plan unfolding as his own work of carving and painting continued. In April 1887 the final building was begun; a sycamore tree was felled and part of the back premises demolished in preparation for the final building in the summer of 1889. Stone arrived from Portland for the new stone staircase on 21st June. This was a very special project and he wished it could have been completed sooner; he had, however, had to wait until he had recouped his costs on the publication of two volumes of the Diary and Letters of his great grandfather (in 1884 and 1886).

On 6th July 1889 scaffolding arrived and part of the house was unroofed and two large sails were laid over the gap in case of weekend-storms. On 1st August he mentioned that the square column for the bottom of the stairs cost £15 12/-. Unfortunately very few of the building costs are given; he states on 27th July that he is paying workmen 6 guineas a week, but there is no record of the number of men employed. On 21st September the highest step of the staircase was placed; the steps had been cut in a shed put up in the garden. A block of Portland stone, four feet square and eight inches thick, was put at the top of the massive staircase. It weighed nearly three-quarters of a ton. 'I like solid building,' he noted, he also observed on 27th September that strangers were apt to look in the windows of the house and ask the housekeeper, 'Is it a church?' He liked to re-assure visiting friends that in spite of their doubts of the steps of the staircase having no support at the outer edge, it was safe.

On 18th January 1890 he wrote, 'the building work is finished at last, last coat of plaster on staircase, but there is still a delay in obtaining the bannister.' On 28th February 1890 three casks of tiles arrived from Godwin of Lugwardine near Hereford, laid by his man in the hall and passage, 'looks very well,' Peter commented.

Work continued inside and entries concerning it continued to the end of the Diary. The walls of the staircase—twenty seven feet three inches in height were painted in a light lavender grey. In July 1890 gothic patterns were impressed at the sides of a doorway; the last operation mentioned is the carving of a grotesque head to go under the mantel shelf in an upstairs room. He wrote that he enjoyed the painting and decorating work in The Old Chancel. Perhaps Ann Newton, his housekeeper enjoyed it less, as she tried to maintain her duties with workmen constantly in the house and Peter always planning new improvements. The last entry concerning his estate was dated 9th June 1894: it became necessary to deepen the well, when the water level was low. This was done in June 1894 and he makes a section drawing.

Peter Hutchinson was a clever maker of models; in July 1891 he writes of those he had made of 4 Coburg Terrace and The Old Chancel. (At a scale of one inch to ten feet). 'Whoever has my houses ought to have my models and my book on The Old Chancel.' Though the houses still stand, the book and the models have vanished.

In December of that year he writes that the recent building operations were an effort to try 'to put my house in order preparatory to my leaving it altogether.'

Literary Enterprises

Peter had literary ambitions from youth, though he destroyed most of his early writing as 'useless' and 'childish'. From the Diary, however, some of the titles can be recovered, and these show the kind of work he was attempting:-

Branscombe Cliffs, a novel of which of wrote; 'my first puerility, published, but one hundred copies burnt.' A five act tragedy of early American history.

Several novels of two or three volumes each. *Terence Crosbie* a five act play (1845). *Busts and Burials in Poets Corner* (1845) concerning the propriety of admitting a statue of Lord Byron to Westminster Abbey.

Three samples of early writing remain: part of the journal written on his walking tour of 1833, and recovered by chance from Staffordshire; also two entries retained from his destroyed Diary which appear at the beginning of volume one of the surviving Diary. The first concerns his voyage home from America by sailing ship in February 1838; the second is the account of the death of his father, Doctor Andrew in 1846.

The Diary gives the titles and authors of the books Peter read, with his comments on them. They cover a wide field; geology, prehistory, archaeology, history, biography, biblical studies, travel, poetry and novels, are all mentioned. Some of his reading was superficial;- on Gibbons' *Decline and Fall of the Roman Empire* he noted—'turned over for an hour or two.' On Risden's *Survey of Devon* he wrote—'skimmed through.' However, on Professor Boyd Hawkins' *Early man in Britain* he declared—'racy, clever, gossiping.'

Data for the *History of the Town, Parish and Manor of Sidmouth* were collected from about 1849. In November 1852 he noted—'began to write a clear and fair copy.' In November 1870 he considered the possibility of publication, but thought it would cost at least £200, and doubted finding two hundred subscribers of £1 each. Geological, archaeological and botanical data were recorded on his many country and beach walks; he noted any changes by land enclosure or coastal erosion, and reported the finding of any rare flower or fern. He drew plans, sections and illustrations for the History and Diary entries. In the coloured sketches there are pictures of houses, local events, wrecked ships and stranded whales. The Diary also contains many newspaper cuttings, and some private letters considered of interest, making a miscellany of records.

Volume one of the History was finished in August 1872. In October 1873 he wrote—'progress is slow, visiting runs away with too much valuable time.' Volume two was finished in August 1875, Volume three in June 1877, Volume four in December 1879 and Volume five in May 1881. There had been many diversions, delays and iterruptions; one of them was Peter's part in translating the Exeter and Exchequer Domesday Books. However, at last the History was finished and laid aside; he was able to write—'the third fair copy completed.'* He thought he would bequeath this, his magnum opus, to the British Museum, with the Diary and Sketches, but in fact he left them to the Exeter Museum and Free Library with other books and papers. Peter had taken interest in the Exeter Museum from its inception, and had given it many items he considered suitable from his curiosities and collections over the years. He wrote that had he been a rich man he would have liked to build a Museum and Free Library for Sidmouth, to which his books would go. Perhaps he hoped for greater recognition in Exeter.

The History begins with a survey of the rock formations and sedimentary deposits which form the local hills and river valleys. There is a large section on prehistory, describing all the hill forts, earthworks, and burial mounds in the neighbourhood, with careful plans and maps. The History then proceeds to documented references to the Manor, Port and Town from medieval times. It is an interesting story and, thanks to Peter's long detailed researches, a very full one. Before the Norman Conquest, the Manor was held with Otterton Manor by Ghyda, widow of Godwin and mother of Harold the King. William the Conqueror granted these manors to the abbey of St. Michael's Mount in Normandy; As Sidmouth was an appendage of Otterton it is not named in the Domesday Book (1086), except in a footnote under Ottery where a saltpan and garden at Sidmouth (Sedemuda) are recorded with the manor held by St. Mary's Cathedral Church in Rouen, which had been given by Edward the Confessor.

A small Priory, for four monks, was founded at Otterton by St. Michael's abbey at the time of King John (1199-1216). Sidmouth manor was then administered by the Priory monks; they must have walked or ridden over Peak Hill by a track, mostly lost by cliff falls, past Cotmaton and down Mill Lane (now All Saints Road) to their mill, on the site now occupied by Ford's shop. There must have been a court house where the tenants came to meet their landlords' representative and pay their dues; the site is lost, but there is extant the Otterton Cartulary, dating from about 1260, preserved by chance in the records of the Duke family of Otterton. At the dissolution of the monasteries in 1539 Richard Duke bought the Priory buildings and built a mansion on the site. He was clerk to the Court of Augmentations which dealt with the sale of monastic property.** The Cartulary gives a list of the Sidmouth tenants and their

---

*The 2nd M.S. copy is in the Devon & Exeter Institution in Exeter.

**Dr. W. G. Hoskins', *Devon,* Otterton, p. 448.

holdings, also a document headed Qualiter Agendum which gives the customs of the manor.

Sidmouth had five sub-manors; Ascerton, Bulverton, Cotmaton, Radway and Woolbrook: their fortunes can be followed in the History., together with other manors held in the district by the abbey, and administered from Otterton. Seized as an Alien Priory in 1415, it was given to Sion Abbey. The abbess leased Sidmouth manor to Richard Gosnell in 1535. Henry VIII took it in 1539 and it was then leased by the Crown, until purchased by Christopher Mainwaring in the 17th century. The manor was then owned and exploited by absentee landlords. The Prideaux family of Netherton Hall in Farway held it for six generations, until, because of financial difficulties, it was put into Chancery in 1787. Later it was sold to Thomas Jenkins of Honiton and Rome. This family also got into legal difficulties and the estate was again in Chancery. It was sold to George Edmund Balfour in 1866. He died in 1869, leaving the estate in the hands of Trustees for his three children. The Trustees built the Manor House, so called, and attempted to improve and enlarge the estate, before the heir came of age.

Peter also made a close study of local documents in the Parish Church chest and in the hands of the Feofees. He translated the Latin documents and listed them all.

The History is illustrated with many pictures of 19th century houses, of the church, before and after its rebuilding, and of the town and the coast. Hubert Cornish's Long View of Sidmouth, both first and second editions (1815 and 1840) are also included, divided into sections.

Peter Hutchinson's other major literary work was the editing of his great grandfather's Diary and Letters, published in two volumes in 1884 and 1886.* On the death of his cousin Canon John Hutchinson of Lichfield, he took over a mass of papers which had come from their common ancestor, Thomas Hutchinson, Governor of Massachusetts; they included copies of letters written by him to members of the Government in Britain at the time of the American Rebellion. Recognising their importance and interest Peter began to sort, study, arrange, and iron out the crumpled muddled collection of documents, diaries and family papers of a hundred or more years before. In November 1882 he queries; 'I wonder whether I am drifting into the compilation of a book?' as indeed he was, with his usual enthusiasm, though he was then 72 years old. He obtained pictures of the Governor and his son the Probate Judge from relatives in America, and went to London several times to consult with the publishers. From the Diary it seems the publication costs for both volumes was about £400 which he later recouped from sales in America and England. Governor Hutchinson had written a three-volume History of Massachusetts Bay; he had also kept a Diary, from which Peter was able to trace his

*A copy is in Sidmouth Museum, for Title Page see p. 59.

ancestors back to Alford in Lincolnshire in the 17th century. In the final chapter of the second volume of the Diary and Letters he gives useful potted biographies of members of the family. Amongst them is an account of the short life of his cousin, Elizabeth Gertrude Oliver, who died in Sidmouth in 1829 aged fifteen. 'A pretty girl and very much admired,' Peter wrote. There is also an account of his father's life as a medical student in Exeter.* Peter published several small books on Sidmouth: *The Geology of Sidmouth* (1843) and *The Ferns of Sidmouth* (1862) among them. His *Guide to Sidmouth* ran to seven editions. He contributed a number of articles to the Transactions of the Devonshire Association and compiled its index for over twenty years. 'A book in the present day is scarcely looked on as complete without an index,' he wrote, as he completed another volume. 'The thing comes easily enough,' he boasted, though his indexes are unhelpful. He took part in a survey on coast erosion by the British Association, which was published in their Report for 1885. He was also the honorary branch secretary for the Society of Antiquaries for thirty years until he resigned in 1889. Peter's writing for other journals, magazines and newpapers continued unabated into his old age. Perhaps there was solace for his increasing loneliness in the familiar routine at The Old Chancel, as he and the 19th century entered their final decade.

*see Extracts pp. 37—39.

Old Age

On his seventieth birthday in 1880 Peter noted in his Diary: 'By temperance and regular living, I have gone on, and I have not had a day's illness for thirty years, and I feel as young as I always did, except that my limbs are not quite as elastic as they were.'

However, by 1884 he began to suffer from bronchitis and sore throat. He called on Doctor Shapter in Exeter several times. In December of that year he 'is grateful for good health and contemplates death with calm resignation that belongs to every Christian believer.'

By November 1885 he began to get anxious: 'I did not venture to church, I am not the boy I was.' On his birthday in that year he notes, 'as a young man I never thought I should attain anything like seventy-five.' In December 1889 he was quite ill with severe rheumatism, bronchitis and sore throat. Doctor Pullin called twice daily for a fortnight; another attack followed in December 1892. He worried about his affairs, often made a new Will, but never felt satisfied he had got it right. Every evening he sat, usually by a fire, reading and writing, and on his long nose he wore the spectacles he had taken to at the age of fifty years and eleven months. His last Will was dated 11th September 1894 a few days after his final Diary entry.

The death of his friends must have added to his isolation. Mr. Heineken, his companion for so many years, died in 1883; he had been failing for some time. Peter was in London when he received a telegram telling of the death. He did not return for the funeral, only noted on 12th August: 'I did not know it was the last time I should see him.' They had worked, jested and played together in their sober way for over forty years. Now the long days of exploring, the exchange of calls and the discussions were over; it must have left a sad gap in Peter's ordered life. Other friends had moved away or had died. Mr Henry Ede of Lansdowne, Elysian Fields, died after a long illness in April 1887; he was buried in the cemetery beside his wife. Peter attended, riding up with Mr. Alured of a new house on Peak Hill in a mourning coach.

Peter Hutchinson's world began to contract; his outings and visits were fewer; the Diary entries diminished in frequency and length; he had become a character in the town: 'Peter the Great', and 'Our Antiquary', he is named on cartoons drawn by Colonel Hawker.* Decorative work went on at The Old Chancel, and his writing continued. As he began to

*in Sidmouth Museum and see frontispiece.

feel his age and suffer from increasing infirmity, he also regretted the lack of near relatives. His brother Bingham's widow and four children were far away in South Australia. He had made a deliberate decision against marriage, but now, too late, he saw the possible advantages of a wife and children. He wrote of his regret at having no family to minister to his needs.

The Vicar, Mr. H. G. J. Clements, who had been in Sidmouth since 1865, and had served as curate before, seems to have been a friend in need to the lonely old man at The Old Chancel. Peter died on 1st October 1897; he was buried in the cemetery to the east and below the chapels. The gravestone is inscribed:

Peter Orlando Hutchinson born 17th November 1810
Baptised Heavitree 2nd October 1811, son of
Andrew Hutchinson, M.D., F.R.C.P., F.R.S., and
his wife Anne Parker daughter of Vice Admiral
Sir William Parker of Harburn Co. Warwick, Bart
In Hope of Eternal Life

There is also a memorial brass in Sidmouth Parish Church, at the east end of the south aisle, 'drawn up by himself on a brass tablet, which he directed to be erected to his memory.' wrote the Vicar.

LIBERTATEM COLO LICENTIAM DETESTOR

PETRUS ORLANDO HUTCHINSON

FIL. ANDRIAE H. DE SIDOST, ET ANNAE (PARKER, DE HARBURN)
FIL. THOMAE H. DE HEAVITREE, ET SARAH (OLIVER, DE BOSTON, MASS.)
FIL. THOMAE H. DE BOSTON, ET HARGARETAE (SANFORD, DE NEWPORT, R.I.)
FIL. THOMAE H. DE EOD.LOC. ET SARAH (FOSTER, AYLESBURY, ENG.)
FIL. ELISHAE H. DE EOD. ET HANNAH (HAWKINS)
FIL. EDWARDI H. DE EOD. ET CATHERINAE (HANBY, DE GIPPEWICO, ENG)
FIL. GULIELMI H. DE ALFORD CO. LINC. ENG. ET. ANNAE (MARBURY)
FIL. EDWARDI H. DE EOD. ET SUSANNAE EJUS UXORIS.
FIL. JOHANNIS H. DE CIVITATE LINC. AT ANNAE UXORIS EJUS

QUI QUIDEM PETRUS NAT. EST WINTON. NOV. 17 1810
BAP HEAVITREE JUXTA EXON OCT. 22 1811
ET OBIIT SIDOST OCT 1 1897

Mr. Clements read a paper on Peter Orlando Hutchinson to the Devonshire Association, meeting in Sidmouth in July 1903.* It gives some account of his life and literary work, of his ability and application; it mentions the spartan conditions at The Old Chancel and his narrow bed, his love for his cat and pet birds, and his cheerful courage in increasing infirmity. Mr. Clements recalled 'how typical an antiquary in aspect in face and figure, in character and demeanour Mr. Hutchinson was. His very handwriting was a copy of the antique, carefully, slowly and elaborately executed; his utterance and diction were equally

*see Transactions of Devonshire Associaton for 1903.

deliberate,' he also noted 'how rapidly and completely he seems to have passed out of recollection.'

Peter Orlando Hutchinson deserves to be remembered with gratitude and acclaim. He was a pioneer of local historical research. His History, Diary and Sketches are a valuable legacy, and an example to other writers—a record of Sidmouth's past for future generations.

Dr. Andrew Hutchinson and his family—

A brief account by his son, Peter

b. on board ship—Mar. 24, 1776.

He was brought to England by his father and mother: bapt. at Kensington, Nov. 6, 1777, as in the Governor's Diary: finished his education at Catherine Hall, University of Cambridge: entered the Medical profession: was articled to Mr. Samuel Luscombe, a surgeon of Exeter—the Articles are dated Feb. 20, 1795. In one of his memorandum books is the following entry:- 'Entered at Cath Hall, Apl. 7. 1796.' At the time when he was a student at Exeter Hospital there was no way of obtaining bodies for dissection but by what some would call rather irregular ways. I have a long copy of verses giving an account of an attempt by the students to disinter a body, when they were attacked by a party of soldiers and driven off. A mem. says—"Written on occasion of an attack made by the Sussex Cavalry on the pupils of the D. and E. Hospital, when disinterring an executed criminal.—Apl. 1796.' I have heard my father say that they went out one night with tools to possess themselves of this body, but had not been digging long before they perceived soldiers in the dim glimmer of the night, getting over the fences, and the discharge of sundry horse-pistols among them, made some of the party rather disposed to run for it:- they however, held their ground, when the soldiers came up, and handling them pretty roughly, for they were evidently the worse for liquor, and threatening them with instant death, thrust their swords through the coats of some, and then led them all off to the Guard Room of the Barracks, where they were temporarily quartered. When there they loudly demanded to see the officers, but the officers were at the Theatre in Exeter. They were released about midnight, but they laid a strong complaint against the conduct of the men in endangering their lives. The officers made every apology, and had the men drawn out in line, when the complainants passed up and down before them, but they found it impossible to identify or swear to any of their assailants.

I have part of the skin of a Negro, hanged about this period at Heavitree gallows, and dissected at the Hospital by my father and the other students. It is however, not so much the skin as the cuticle and colouring matter. It is of a deep brown.

The use of hair powder was at this time general, and frequent mention of it occurs in his cash-book.

1799, Nov. 15,	Powder and pomat,	1.6,
1800, Ap. 5	Powder Certificate	1.1.0,
1801, Feb. 20	Powder puff	2.0

I remember the powder puff. It was an oblate ball of swan's down about as big as a man's fist, with a short handle on the upperside, and kept in a round wooden box, (I still have the box) with the hair powder. I have often seen him powder his hair by dabbing this puff against it. When I was a child I one day saw him bathe. He dived into the water with his head white, and he came up with his head black—greatly to my astonishment.

The cost of his Degree was this:-

Expenses for degree, etc.,			
1801, March 26 Gretton's men		8	6
Professor for Act	7	7	0
Caution	1	0	0
University servants		10	0
Registrar	4	5	0
Proctor	2	10	10
College fees	6	19	4
	£23	0	8

He was elected one of the Physicians of Exeter Hospital in or about Oct. 1801 at the early age of 25, and a Fellow of the Royal Society in May 1804, and an entry referring to it appears thus:-

May 3, Admission fees, &c., to Royal Society £6 0 0

He had a brass door plate made, with his name, 'Dr. Hutchinson' engraved on it, (which I still have) which is thus recorded:-

1801, June 4, Door Plate 0 9 0.

Further on appears the following:-

1804, Dec. 24, Admiss. and Subs to London Med. Society £3 3 0

He resigned his appointment at Exeter Hospital in Feb. 1804, went to London, lectured on medical subjects and married, October 29 1805, Anne, daughter of Vice Admiral Sir William Parker, of Harburn, Co. Warwick, Bart., whose widow had a house on Ham Common in the parish of Kingston-upon-Thames. The following entry—'1805, Oct. 9, Wg. ring 0,,7,,6' I doubt not is the Wedding ring. Though one of the best of mothers has now been 30 years in her grave I have got this ring, and also the guard-ring that she wore over it. The other entries are plain:

'25th, Marriage Licence	3	3	0
29th, Clergyman	5	0	0
Clerk	0	10	6
Ringers and Sexton	1	10	6
Lady P's servants,	2	10	6

He lived for a time at Richmond, in Surrey; was appointed Physician to Winchester Hospital: returned to Devonshire, and eventually died at Sidmouth, Dec. 23, 1846. His widow, who was born June 12, 1778, died at Sidmouth March 5, 1855, having had issue—

1) Young Bingham (Godfathers, Mr. Young and Admiral Bingham) b. at Richmond, Surrey Aug. 14 and bapt. Oct. 14, 1806. He was a good classical scholar, with a quick turn for figures and mathematical studies. He entered the Royal Navy at the usual age, but after some years' service, and having a strong passion for emigration, he joined the first expedition for founding the projected colony of South Australia; and as Cap. Sir John Hindmarsh, the first Governor, had known his uncle the second Sir W. P., he went out in the same ship with him in or about 1835. When there, he joined the exploring parties that searched the country for a good place for the Capital. Influenced by Sir John, who inclined to think that near the mouth of the great river Murray would be the most advantageous place for the capital city, as opening up a highway to the heart of the country, he bought near 1,000 acres at Goolwa, Port Eliot, and the Hindmarsh Valley; but the next Governor decided to place the chief city where Adelaide now stands. He returned to England; married Augusta Kingdon, of Narracot, June 15. 1852, at Heavitree; sailed again Nov. 5 in the same year, and busied himself on his estates until his death, which occurred Aug. 3, 1870.

2) Elizabeth Louisa, b. at Richmond Jun. 2. 1808 bapt. Sept. 10, d. Mar. 11. 1809.

3) Louisa Anne: b. at Richmond June 26, 1809, bapt. Oct. 8, and d. Mar. 10, buried Mar. 12, 1810, in the parish of St. Laurence, Winchester.

4) Peter Orlando, b. at Winchester, Nov. 10, 1810, bapt. at Heavitree Oct. 22, 1811 (The Editor)

5) Frances Harriet, b. at Tiverton, Devon, Apr. 24, 1812, bapt. at St. Peter's church, May 21, 1813; m. Charles, eldest son of Gen. Rumley of Arcot House, Sidmouth, July 18, 1838, at Tiverton. He d. in S. Australia Mar. 4, 1855, buried at Gawlertown. She m. 2ndly Mr. John Robertson, widower, of Strowan Grove, near Salisbury, S.A., in 1856. He d. 1870.

6) William George, b. at Tiverton, July 18, and bapt. Aug. 28, 1813. He d. Ap. 6. and buried at St. George's Chapel, Fore Street, Ap. 11, 1822.

(From *Diary and Letters* Some account of Governor Hutchinson's family, vol. II, p. 474)

Death of Dr. Andrew Hutchinson—1846

Friday Dec. 25, Christmas Day. Received the following letter from my brother:-

Sidmouth 24 Dec. 1846 'My dear Peter,—

Your father died yesterday at 6 p.m. and it is my mother's particular wish that you come down to the funeral, which is to take place here on Tuesday, if possible. You, and my mother are named as Executor and Executrix; and £500 are left to you, as well as half of section 18 (at Alexandria, Victor Harbour, South Australia; being the plot of 134 acres bounded on the east by the river Hindmarsh, and on the south by the sea). As I am bothered with business and have many letters to write, it is not necessary to say more, as we expect you so soon.

I am your affectionate Brother, Bingham Hutchinson.'

On the receipt of the above, I made immediate preparations for the journey. I excused myself from Mr. Green's Xmas party, but without alleging the reason, and went to the Paddington station to enquire about the departure of trains.

Saturday Dec. 26.—Got on the rail at Paddington at a quarter before ten, and was taken by the Express train to Exeter in four hours and a half—distance I think 194 miles. As I had two or three hours to spare I walked out to Heavitree where my uncles and cousins have been buried to enquire the particulars in case my father should be buried there, as I was disposed to wish for. Learnt from Atherley, the Vicar, that in the vault in the church my grandfather, Judge Hutchinson, and his wife were buried, but I forget whether there were any others; but since the erection of the new church, burials are not allowed to take place—not even in the old vaults. In common graves, about twelve yards west of the north-west corner of the churchyard close against the wall that bounds the lane, in a cluster are Thomas Hutchinson, son of the Judge, William his younger brother, formerly curate of this parish; Louisa, William's wife, and Henrietta, their child. At William's feet lies Thomas's son William, but without a monument. It was my wish that my father should be near them; but two days before his death he said he might as well be buried at Sidmouth.

(From the first Diary pages retained from earlier destroyed Diary)

A visit to a Pottery and a Coal Mine—Extracts from a Journal by Peter Orlando Hutchinson

The Pottery—Longton 1833

Through the kindness and influence of a gentleman at Blurton I enjoyed the gratification of a thorough inspection of an establishment in going over which my satisfaction at observing the contrivances, the novel methods (to me) by which the result is aimed at, and finally the quickness with which the operations are performed and terminated was no less great than pleasing.

The white clay—the chief ingredient in almost everything they make, though not the sole one, is mostly brought from the vicinity of Chudleigh in Devonshire. I have often seen it dug there myself. There is a great deal of trouble bestowed on it before the artisans can manufacture it into whatever article may be desired. It is first thrown into a pit with water, and in that kept continually stirred and agitated to dissolve it entirely. It is then passed through a succession of lawn sieves which reduces it to a state perfectly smooth and impalpable. Other things that require grinding, such as flint, colours and various others, are submitted to a mill, the lower stones of which are made of trap rocks brought from Wales, while the upper or those that revolve immediately on them are of a softer nature, and come from Derbyshire. The clay is likewise, in its maximum of humidity, thrown into another pit and boiled for a considerable time, after this it is taken out and rendered sufficiently thick to allow of working . . .

The Coal Mine October 1833

The gentleman whose influence obtained me this gratification through the potteries, likewise got me the opportunity of descending a coal pit if I could say my heart was stout enough to bid me undertake it. Certainly, I said, rather surprised at the question, for the thought of fear about such a thing had never entered my imagination. The next day, October 13th, was appointed for the undertaking, and I did not fail to be at the proprietors in time, whose house stood a few yards from the mouth of the pit.

The perpendicular depth of the shaft before arriving at the horizontal passages, measures the immense number of 720 feet. At the bottom of this in one of the excavations near it, there is a powerful steam engine employed to draw coals up an inclined plane of 1,800 feet deeper—only fancy, 1,800 feet deeper!

This is one of the deepest pits in the kingdom, and I was told the circumstance of the engine so far underground is supposed to be without parallel.

I dressed myself in a kind of flannel covering and then we made for the pit. The cleanest wagon was selected (whose sides were a long inch thick with mud mixed with coal dust) and it was slung over the hole. The size of the wagon was 3½ feet in length and in width 3. We stepped into it and were suspended, (suppose the rope breaks now, thought I—only 720 feet). The signal was given and we descended. My stomach gave an indescribable turn when the support to my feet gave way and sank under me . . . We descended at a prodigious rate for a long time, until at last day light came to day darkness, and after that it was difficult to see, we possessing human eyes. In this state of affairs I felt we were not stationary by the jolting of our vehicle; though now having become habituated to the sinking motion I could scarcely tell which way we were travelling, up or down . . . After we had been in the dark for a week (perhaps less) I had the curiosity to ask my guide how far down he thought we were;

'Oh, 'bout half way, Sir'.

We went on again rumble, rumble, rumble, for I durst not say how long, till I began to think we could be but a little way from the centre of the globe; indeed I supposed we were, for he soon began to bellow to the men below to 'take care' what they were about and make way for the jinnleman.'

I now bent my knees a trifle to ease the expected concussion for I did not know the moment we should alight in Pandemonium. Scarcely had I made the preparation when down we came—bang. We got out somehow or other and I was then told to stoop and crawl under a cross beam or lintel, as it were, and not remain under the aperture for fear lest anything should by accident fall down . . . What with coming down so far in the waggon, creeping about before I had time to collect myself and the darkness of everything around me, I was so dizzy, bewildered and giddy that my new companions made me sit down as they plainly saw I could not stand . . . Numerous candles were now lighted, the black gloom was somewhat dissipated and hell began to look less hellish. Some were stuck against the sides of projecting pieces of rock by the aid of lumps of clay; and we each held one of those humble torches in our hands. Now we began to proceed along a passage running westward, but the roof was so low that to accomplish it we were obliged first of all to double ourselves up in a zig-zag fashion, just as a large map is folded in an octave volume. After crawling along this for about sixty or eighty feet the tunnel divided in two: the left going on westward, and the right, which we took, keeping somewhat toward the north of west. Here we crawled again in a most break-back and compact posture conceivable—as flat on the ground as a cat may be observed creeping across a lawn when a sparrow has pitched on the grass a few yards ahead of her. In the midst of this uncomfortable mode of travelling my candle went out—but that was a trifle in affairs of the nation. At the next divergence of the passage we once more took the right hand direction turning sharp round to the east. Here we had to ascend a steep hill for a much longer space of time than was either sublime or rapturous. On one side there ran down a gurgling and limpid stream of water—a most happy and poetical circumstance elsewhere. The path was only two or three inches deep in mud of a very singular species and possessed of remarkable qualities . . . To keep on one's legs was out of the question. It was nothing but slipping, sliding, stumbling and falling upon one's hands from the bottom the whole way up to the top. In this adventure my poor candle had been marred grievously. Its flame had precipitately forsaken it sometime before; but by falling on my hands so often I had buried this creature no less often in the mud and had squeezed it to pieces in the most pitiless manner. On attaining the summit of this tedious ascent, near the top of which it took a bend to the left, we entered a squarish cavern about twelve of fifteen feet across its greatest length, but scarcely high enough anywhere to allow of standing upright. The exertion of creeping through these confused passages in so uncomfortable and doubled a posture; the stagnation, impurity and oppressive heat of the atmosphere were altogether too powerful to be borne. When I got to this cavern I was so overcome by the effects of all these that I experienced sensations too dreadful to describe; I never fainted in my life—no not even now but I verily believe I pretty well learnt what the feel must be. I was dizzy, sickish and half unconscious of what passed round me. Breathing was painfully difficult, and the great heat of the place was rendering the candles quite soft and oily. In a nearly insensible state I have some recollection of crying out for fresh air, but I may as well have cried for the light of the sun. Quite exhausted, I involuntarily sank down on a heap of coals, where I remained more than half an hour to recover myself . . . The workmen however, appeared of another nature quite; they were singing, telling comic stories and joking; they were seemingly just as happy as if daylight had been shining on them, and as if seven hundred feet of solid earth had not been impending close over their heads.

To avoid the slippery and dirty descent of the passage in returning from thence, I was placed on a kind of small sledge: and when I was put on top of the hill and pushed out over, I glided down in the dark at a glorious rate. Instead of at once going to the shaft where we alighted we went to the commencement of the long inclined plane, 1,800 feet deep, as I said before; it is possible to walk down this but it is very difficult. The coals are drawn up in wagons by the steam engine, and to descend in such a vehicle is the best way, but I was dissuaded from this tedious journey as my curiosity was so far satisfied: and, moreover, it was thought by all parties that I was deep enough already.

After remaining here for the greater portion of an hour to observe what was going on, we went back as we had come, passed under the shaft and proceeded about thirty yards further until we stood before Old Pluto . . . The engine was in full play—the furnace red hot—and the hissing steam that escaped rendered the place like a brewhouse. To describe the heat here is more than I shall attempt. The demon-like workmen had nothing on but shoes and trousers; from their waists upward they were entirely bare and they were in so profuse a state of perspiration that where it did not positively run down their backs, it stood on them in hanging drops of dew. At this situation I put a piece of coal in my pocket as a relic, and soon after joyfully stepped into the waggon to ascend. A steam engine in the open air above drew us up, for the other is at work at the incline. The effect of again coming into daylight was most curious and perplexing. Everything was too glaring to look at and the colouring of the surrounding scene was strange and striking. Finally I found myself once more in the world after having been out of it for more than an hour and a half.

(Contributed by Mr. Rodney Hampson of Newcastle Lodge, Keele, Newcastle, Staffordshire. June 1980).

Concerning the paper above read to North Staffordshire Field Club—2/3/1915 and published in the Club Transactions about Peter Orlando Hutchinson's walking tour in 1833.

The Rev. S. W. Hutchinson read extremely interesting extracts from the journal of a walking tour made by his father's cousin and contemporary Peter Orlando Hutchinson in 1833. He started from Sidmouth and walked 1,237 miles through England and Wales. The journal of the tour is itself a remarkable document in the author's own handwriting, beautifully illustrated with a number of sketches. It must have taken many weeks for the writer to record his impressions, and his carefully noted experiences are now of considerable value. The extracts read by Mr. Hutchinson dealt with:

1. A railway journey from Liverpool to Manchester
2. A visit to a Lane End (Longton) Pottery
3. A descent into a coal mine

Mr. Hutchinson said the writer was a south-country man who had never seen a train before, or a coal mine.

The President said:- "The Manchester to Liverpool line was the first one made and it was interesting to hear the description of the difficulties encountered. They must remember there were no buffers in those days and there was no glass in the windows. He remembered how, when he was a boy, the family made the journey from Norton Bridge to North Wales. The luggage was always put on the top of the carriage in which they were sitting, and it was necessary to have a ladder for the purpose.'

Mr. Hutchinson said he had no doubt that John Harvey of Blurton House, was the gentleman who arranged the visits to the coal mine and pottery, but he could not identify the manufactory or colliery.

Mr. G. A. Mitcheson said it would be one of Mr. Sparrows collieries, the old No. 8 or Railway Pit in all probability.

(Contributed by Mr. Rodney Hampson as mentioned above).

Home by Sailing Ship from New York—1838

New York—1 Feb. 1838

At 11 a.m. got on board the London Packet ship *Mediator*. At noon we hove off from the wharf at the foot of Pine Street, and the steamer tow-boat took us out beyond Sandy Hook. The day was wonderfully mild—the bay almost wholly without floating ice—and we all (us passengers) stood on the deck to admire the scenery, and see the last of New York. Just ahead of us the Havre packet was being towed out and astern came the packet for Liverpool. (We saw neither of these all the way over the Atlantic although we all arrived at our several ports within a few days of each other). As the sun went down, we saw the last of the New World—I believe the Heights near the Narrows—and then the land vanished like a grey cloud on the horizon. Now when we are fairly off—the 'Skipper' or 'Old Man' says we shall be in England in eighteen days; but as I was 49 coming out, this appears too fair a hope. An uncomfortable evening, nothing in order.

On the Atlantic—18 Feb. 1838

Lord Bacon says that it is a very foolish thing for a man at sea to sit down and write a diary of events which happen during a voyage: for, as he says, every succeeding day must be like the preceding, and a record of events is only ringing changes on some half dozen things which regularly occur in succession.

Today the wind blew from the northern and we went along 'like winking'—but 'oh horror' as Fanny Kemble says, I got sea sick—yes I did, 'and no mistake'. It is just a twelvemonth since I made my last voyage but I have had a great deal of boating, both in travelling and in excursions in my own boat at Boston; so that I had almost flattered myself that my sea horrors were over for ever. I suffered for ten days coming out.

Straits of Dover—27 Feb. 1838

Wind easterly during this morning—fell calm toward noon, and in the afternoon it sprung up to the south-west—this is better. However, we made very little way, and got no glimpse of land, though we are coming up towards the Straits.

Fell in with and spoke to a Hamburg schooner.

After tea drove away the evening with a game of Speculation.

28 Feb. 1838

Took in a third pilot this morning.

At 7 a.m. obtained a good view of Dover—the castle—and Shakespeare's Cliff. How often have I seen Dover in this way—in steamers, packets and various sorts of craft—and yet I never was there. I fancy I know all about the castle hill, and the fine cliff, off which Lear was going to jump, and yet forsooth I never was on either. Towards the evening we ran by Margate with a fair wind, for it is gradually veering round to the west. We were a long time making short tacks, as we arrived nearer the Thames. Several large ships were in our case; but we beat them all in sailing—these American packets are beautiful sailers. We passed

Chatham and the hulls of six large ships on the stocks were visible. As the sun went down we cast anchor for the night, for the skipper was afraid of proceeding in the dark.

Turned into bed about ten, and thought it very queer that now I was so near treading again on the soil of Old England—a much better soil than the Yankees can boast of. True, there are many things which I like in America—but then there are many more which I prefer in England.

Thames and London 1 March 1838

At 4 a.m. was awoke by a steamboat coming alongside and fastening herself to us, to give us a lift up the river. Slept again till 7. Turned out—breakfast, shave-polish up—passed the towns merrily. What a very antique and venerable look there is about every building in this country, when compared with the newness shed over everything in the one I have just left. Quite astonished to find they have had so severe a winter in England: the winter in America has been the mildest one almost ever known.

Entered the St. Catherine's Dock and went ashore.

Quite horrified in walking through Cornhill, to see that the Royal Exchange had been burnt down. It happened while I was in the middle of the Atlantic, about a fortnight ago. What a pity!

(P.O.H. wrote before the entry dated December 25 1846 'All my Diary for 15 years previous to this, I have burnt as being useless.' But he did retain 'Home by sailing ship' and 'Death of Dr. Andrew Hutchinson', both reprinted above).

Ducks and Drakes—31. Jul. 1849

Poor 'Mr. Tommy', the white drake, makes a disconsolate widower. He and his wife, 'Mrs. Tommy', were sitting as usual under the currant bushes, after being tired of walking about looking for slugs, when Mrs. T., who had not been very well for several days, very quietly leant her head forward and died. The drake was found sitting beside her perfectly contented, but was very loth to go to roost without her in the evening. All the next day, (Saturday) she was left in the same position, and it was amusing to see with what complaicency (sic.) he sat beside her. In the evening, however, it was decided that she must be buried; and in order to convince Mr. Tommy that his wife had not been stolen from him by the hand of man, but that she was really dead, he was present at the solemnity, and he was even put into the grave on his wife before she was covered, that he might know what had become of her. This seems to have had a salutary effect, for although he appears disconsolate, he does not wander about the premises to search for her. She was not above eight years old; but about a month ago we were abliged to kill an old duck 'Mrs. Mooty', which must have been upwards of 20. Mrs Mooty was roughly used by the Muscovy duck (not Mr. Tommy), otherwise she might have lived on. My sister had her eight years; the Rev. Prebendary Dornford, of Plymtree, had her eleven and before that she had been brought from Italy, a full grown duck. I should think that twenty years is an advanced period for a duck.

(From the Diary).

Wedding Occasion I

18th Sept. 1849—Captain Creighton and Miss Ann Fitzgerald.

Bingham and myself breakfasted with the Creightons at 1 Coburg Terrace, and then went to Captain Creighton's wedding at Sidbury. His bride, Miss Ann Fitzgerald, eldest daughter of Major Fitzgerald of Mount Edgar, was more courageous than himself on the occasion. I have heard that the ladies are generally so on such occasions, though I don't know why. She answered 'I will' to the clergyman's question very firmly. We had a splendid breakfast afterwards at Major Fitzgerald's where I had to make a speech and propose the health of the bridesmaids. It is said to have been long the custom for the gentlemen to kiss the bridesmaids at weddings; but whether the times are changed or whether it is owing to the growth of real modesty, or mock modesty, I don't know, but it seems to be falling into disuse. However, in order that the ladies should know that I had not forgotten the custom, I filled my pockets with those bon-bons called 'kisses' and these I distributed liberally. The practice of clapping hands and knocking the table after drinking toasts is very properly being discontinued in decent society. It is said that the Queen has expressed her dislike to so much noise as she has heard made, when her health has been drunk at public dinners; and perhaps it is to this that we owe a better state of things.

Altogether the party went off admirably. When the bride and bridegroom drove away, Major Fitzgerald threw a shoe after them 'for good luck'. What is the origin of this custom?

19 Sept. 1849

Today was kept as a day of fasting and humiliation, to endeavour to avert the divine anger which has come upon us in the form of cholera. At church with my mother—the congregation was numerous.

(From the Diary).

Wedding Occasion II

2 Dec. 1852. Lieut. Darnell and Miss Emily FitzGerald.

This morning Miss Emily FitzGerald, daughter of Major FitzGerald of Mount Edgar, was married to Lieut. I Darnell. I was at her sister's wedding in September 1849. I was told I behaved very badly today. I borrowed a horn and blew it out of the carriage window all the way to Sidbury (three miles) and all the way back again; the ceremony went off very well in Sidbury church, though the ring was a little too small. I asked Miss Emily whether she was not in an immense fright, to which she answered;—'only a little shaky'.

We had a capital breakfast at Mount Edgar, and sat down about twenty. I was between Mrs. Jenkins of Lime Park and Miss Amelia Elphinstone. I have since made a coloured drawing of the scene in the church, and given it to the Major.

(From the Diary).

The Perils of Coach Travel

22 Oct. 1850

Tuesday Oct. 22—Went into Exeter by the mail. When we were within a mile and half of Ottery, the horses ran away and we were turned over. John Hook, marker at the Billiard Room, jumped off and broke one of his legs very badly just above the ankle. We then ran on nearly a quarter of a mile, and were all pitched into a garden on the left side. If we had been thrown against a house or a wall, our brains must have been dashed out on the spot. I lighted on the hedge upon my back, and unhurt. A woman made a grasp at the luggage to save herself, but by mistake caught hold of the guard's key bugle, and then flew over me. Dr. Marsh's groom had his green livery coat torn from the skirts up to the collar, and presented the most ludicrous appearance. Everybody was more or less hurt but myself. When we were all righted and ready to proceed, one of the passengers, a lady, was so fearful that no intreaties or arguments from the coachman or passengers could make her take her place. It is said that a joke will prevail where a sober argument will sometimes be urged in vain. I tried it: 'Madam,' said I. 'You never heard of a coach being turned over twice in one day.' The remark was convincing. Everybody burst out laughing and the lady got in.

Sun. Oct. 27: Dr. Cullen called on me to offer his congratulations on my escape from the coach last Tuesday. My narrative is in Woolmer (newspaper).

(From the Diary).

***In Loco Parentis* at Uffculme—**

18. Jan. to 11 Mar. 1851

Went to Exeter by the mail via Ottery without being turned over. Called at Dr. Oliver's and left him some casts of the Roman coin, and some impressions of the inscription on the 4th bell at Sidmouth . . . On to

Uffculme, taking the rail as far as the Tiverton Junction. Arrived at the School House about four, and found the Joneses well . . .

24 Jan. The Joneses started this morning for Leamington, Warwickshire, leaving me to look after 5 children and 4 maidservants for the next 10 days. After the children had had their tea, had a good romp, making noise enough to tear the house down, and gone to bed, I enjoyed a little peace, first having an hour at the piano and, then reading Layard's *Nineveh.*

27 Jan. Had breakfast, fed the cat, fed the pigs, set the children to needlework; nursed the baby; carved for the whole of them at dinner; sent them out on the green to play; had them all for tea; then after half an hour's riotous play was somewhat relieved by the appearance of the nursemaid who took them off to bed . . .

2 Feb. Sunday—At church twice with the children. Uffculme church is unusually handsome for a small country town . . .

3 Feb. Mr. and Mrs. Jones returned from their visit to Leamington and Worcester. Gladly returned the keys to their hands before the children had succeeded in dethroning me and setting up a republic . . .

11 Mar. Left Uffculme for Sidmouth. Called on Mr. J. Norris and C. F. Williams in Exeter.

(From the Diary).

Mules and Music at a Picnic

2 Aug. 1858

Though not recovered from my weary week in Exeter,* I went to a picnic on Dunscombe Cliffs—a very pretty place, where I have not been for some years. We built a fire place with stones, collected wood, and boiled our kettle out of doors. We did more, we boiled our potatoes for dinner beautifully. We dined on the hill; we sang songs and I accompanied them on the flute; and then I gave them some lively tunes, and set them dancing on the grass. We rambled about, down to the beach at Weston, and up again; boiled the water and had tea. During this time, the lads who drove us had wandered away; so that when we wanted to pack up and go home there was no-one to assist. We therefore had to do everything ourselves. There was some difficulty in catching the mules. Some of the party drove them into a corner, whilst I and others were engaged in collecting the tea things and packing them away. Whilst I was so engaged, and had a tea pot and cream jug in my left hand, I saw that one of the mules was going to make a bolt and run away; so I went before him to stop him; but he turned, and let out his heels at me, and very dexterously kicked the tea pot out of my hands and sent it flying. It was a

*on Jury service

most absurd event. It might have been a serious one; but as it happened, it was a very laughable one. As the lads had not come back, I drove home one carriage, and Frederick Walker (of Lime Park) another. They overtook us, running at a great pace, just as we were near Sidmouth.

(From the Diary).

To Osborne to Visit the Queen

23 Mar. 1860.

Attended a vestry meeting of a very stormy kind: from the church (or, rather, the Tower, for the church is not finished), we adjourned to the Town Hall. An address recently issued by the Rev. the Earl of Buckinghamshire, discouraging the putting up of certain tractarian symbols in the church, and advising the parishioners to attend and vote against them, brought a large attendance. Although one of the Building Committee I have felt latterly that I could not pull with the other members. I felt I sided more the the Earl's view rather than those of the Committee. It was a most unpleasant thing for me today, to make a speech condemnatory of the course now proposed to be taken by those gentlemen with whom I have worked for fifteen months. When the votes were taken, the parish (including the Earl's view and mine) had a majority of four to one over the Tractarians.

14 Sept. The Earl was twice at my house about it today.

17 Sept.

Having received a letter from the E. I was an hour with him this afternoon. Also an hour with Dr. Newman.

18 Sept.

The E. was with me an hour this morning in The Old Chancel.

19 Sept.

Left Sidmouth for Osborne House, Isle of Wight, where the Queen is staying for a few days, having with me a memorandum referring to some curious proceedings about our church, from the E., which her Majesty ought to know. Up at half past five—breakfast at six—and on the coach at half past six for Honiton. Took the new line of rail recently opened, from Honiton via Sherborne to Salisbury and Southampton. Got immediately into a steamer, and arrived at Cowes about 3 p.m. At the Hotel I immediately changed my dress to my uniform, and found the use of it. Sentries presented arms, and the Queen's gatekeeper threw the portal open wide as he saw me approach. As I walked through the park, a pony carriage with a girl of six or eight years old in it, led by a groom, in the Royal Livery, crossed the road about 100 yards ahead of me. It was one of the little princesses. Osborne House is in a plain Italian style. When the Queen bought the property of Lady . . . some years ago, the old house was pulled down and the present one built. The park is nearly the same as before, with some improvements, but several farms have been bought near it, so that the estate now amounts as I was told, to nearly 7,000 acres. My uniform had the same effect at the house. The footman did not wait till I had knocked. I had a long talk with Major Elphinstone, tutor to Prince Arthur, and I am to call again tomorrow.

Returned to West Cowes, and got something to eat and drink for I now had a right to feel hungry, having had nothing for exactly twelve hours and travelled and walked a few miles into the bargain.

20 Sept.
Fine morning, at eleven girt on my sword and walked out again. Was nearly an hour with Major Elphinstone (whose father and family reside near Sidmouth) and pen, ink and paper having been brought to me by one of the footmen, I wrote a note to Col. the Hon. Sir Charles Phipps, her Majesty's secretary, enclosing the petition to the Queen, which I had brought with me. The prayer of the petition asks for enquiry into some of our church matters, and I was informed that it would be acted upon.

Having therefore, performed the objects of my mission I prepared to return. Awaiting the steamboat, I took a walk about Cowes, and admired the many pretty yachts on the water. Left Cowes at six: steamed past Calshot Castle, and arrived at Southampton about half past seven.

21 Sept.
Having slept at Southampton, I took the rail at 9 a.m. I recognised Sir John Bowring at the station. He had been giving some lectures at Southampton. I returned by the same route, via Salisbury and Yeovil to Honiton. On the Sidmouth coach I rode over the hill, but got down short of Sidmouth, and quietly reported myself to the Earl of Buckinghamshire as having returned. I then walked home.

22 Sept.
The Earl surprised me at 10 a.m. this morning, to talk over my recent mission and arrange future plans. The Rev. H. Gibbes, Incumbent of All Saints, likewise was with me, the Earl having admitted him into his confidence. My other book, on the Restoration of Sidmouth Church, contains some other particulars about this business.

27 Sept.
The Earl has just given me two or three things to put in my Old Chancel—a great mass of petrified moss; two stuffed birds, Ruffs &c. some coins; a piece of magnetic iron &c.

(From the Diary)

Belbury Castle Discovered

May 31. 1861:-

Started with Mr. Heineken for an antiquarian expedition on Aylesbeer Hill &c and to look for Belbury Castle—for which we have been enquiring for a dozen years. We drove to Newton Poppleford, where we got out. We examined the government mark left by the officers of the Ordnance Survey, in the northwest corner of the pretty little tower, and took observations with a sympiesometer we had with us. The mark is in the broad arrow beside a copper bolt driven into a large stone, with a horizontal slit, being at 132.8 feet above the level of mean tide. The service was going on. I looked into the church: there was nobody there but the parson and clerk . . .

Thence we proceeded to look for Belbury Castle. After some trouble we found its site near 'Brick House' between two and three miles south-west of Ottery or near The Schools. On the flank of the hill, in the plantation, there is a very remarkable sunk road. From Belbury Castle it can be traced all the way north to Streetway Head. Before the land was enclosed it was perfect, but even now is visible. All our doubts were set at rest by falling in with an old man of 79 called Samuel White who lives at Castle Farm. He told us that 70 years ago, when he was a boy, the land was wild heath, that he and his father assisted in levelling the earthworks round the camp—that they raised the earth in the middle of the camp from what they got at the banks round it—that there was a great ditch all round outside the bank—that the present road round the south and east sides, occupies the bottom of the former ditch—that he never heard of any coins, or weapons or other relics, ever having been found in the camp, that the camp was called Belbury, or Belsbury Castle—and that the field now occupying its site is known as Castle Field. He also told us that he had traced the sunk road all the way to Streetway Head, and could point out many portions of it even now.

(From the Diary).

A Christmas Crinoline Ball

Dec. 19. 1862

Went to the Christmas Ball at half past nine this evening at the London Inn Sidmouth. Gentlemen's tickets 7/6, Tea, refreshments, and supper difficult to get at, and uncomfortable to take. What is most remarkable in the present day, and equally absurd is the size of the ladies' dresses. Their crinoline petticoats, extended with steel hoops, have attained dimensions quite ridiculous. Because it is the fashion it is tolerated; but even the ladies admit the absurdity, and wish the Empress of the French (who makes and maintains fashions for the whole world) would be so good as to reduce the size. I remarked one young lady, seated on a row of chairs, and she and her dress covered three chairs and a half. And as they are as unnecessarily long as they are unnecessarily wide, sweeping the ground as they go, it is most difficult to walk near them or after them without stepping on their skirts or flounces. Very laughable were the jams and collisions that often took place by the rapid, too rapid twirling of the waltzes. Sometimes one was suddenly enveloped in sundry huge clouds of muslin or silk, by the meeting together around one of several of these roving and spinning couples inadvertently converging to one point; and then off they were again in an instant to the four corners of the universe—or room. Towards the latter part of the evening, it was amusing to see strips of blue, red or white muslin or shreds of silk, which had been trod off or torn off by collisions, lying on the floor or driven about by the whirlwind of these fleet revolvers. Quadrilles, Lancers and polkas were the other dances, I got home at a quarter to four.

(From the Diary).

Sylvan Picnics

Jun. 24. 1863

About twenty of us had a very agreeable Pic-nic in Harpford Wood:—the Vanes, Gardiners, Dillons, &c. The weather was beautiful. We have so far had a finer, drier, and warmer summer this year than any year since 1859. We drove in carriages to the Wood, which mostly consists of beech trees, and contains, according to the country people, as many acres of land as there are days in a year—365. After we had enjoyed a very good dinner, spread on the ground, we dispersed and rambled about. I went with some friends down to Harpford village and called on the elder Gardiners. Again in the wood, we had tea and chatted till it was time to return home.

May. 16. 1874:

Had a pleasant Pic-nic party in Harpford Wood with General and Mrs. and Miss Alice Balmain of Camden, and Mrs. Ritchie and five of her children of the Balsters. The wood was very beautiful, but it is rather too early in the season yet. Had both our dinner and tea under the trees. Rambled from the Keeper's Cottage down to the great embankment of the railway, at the head of the narrow little meadows. Dug up fern roots and seedling oaks and beeches; and home.

(From the Diary).

An Ecclesiastical Bargain

15 Dec. 1863:—

Went over to Awliscombe to look after an old church window. Ever since I erected the 'Old Chancel' I have contemplated adding to it in the same antique style and thereby converting the whole affair into a residence. Took coach to Honiton, nine miles, and then walked out two further to the village. The large window of the south transept has been taken out and replaced by a new one . . . The pieces of the window taken out were lying in the S.E. Corner of the churchyard . . . Wanting to see the churchwarden, Mr. Banfield, about the window I walked a mile further to Wadhay. Mr. Banfield told me he understood the old window was worth £6 but that I might have it for £5. Did not then conclude any bargain. Walked back to Honiton and took the coach to Sidmouth . . .

28 Dec.

Mr. Wm. Banfield, churchwarden of Awliscombe, came over on business, and called on me at 9 a.m. He had breakfast with me. We concluded our bargain about our church window. I gave him £4 and conditionally one more if worth it.

29 Dec.—

John White, the carrier, with his waggon and two horses, went over to Awliscombe and brought over about half of the great stone window, S. Churchill, stone cutter, accompanied him.

(From the Diary)

The Devonshire Association is Entertained at Knowle

(Meeting at Sidmouth in July 1873)

A brilliant finish was given by the invitation extended to the Members by R. N. Thornton, Esq. Although away from home, Mr. Thornton telegraphed to the Local Secretary to invite the Members to luncheon, at his beautiful residence at Knowle. Accordingly, at the conclusion of the ordinary business most of the Members repaired thither, and were certainly delighted with the beauty of the scene and the hospitality shown them. All that many days, and even nights, of zealous labour could do was done to add to the attraction of the beautiful spot by liberally exercising the hand of improvement wherever required. The house is one of the quaintest in the county, and the grounds and gardens exceedingly beautiful. The visitors were enthusiastic in their admiration of the radiant Italian garden; the rosery; the rockery, with its foundations flashing into spray in the summer sunshine; the palaces of glass, in which rare plants and flowers bloom and delicious fruit is produced. The Members of the Association were entertained at a most recherché luncheon laid out in a tent on the grounds, and altogether their reception was exceedingly gratifying. The Sidmouth band enlivened the scene with some excellent music.

(From Transactions of the Devonshire Association p. 360 1874).

Comedy on Hembury Fort

22 Aug. 1874:—

From an invitation from Miss Venn, who was at Sidmouth a few days ago, we went today. We took the rail to the Junction, where she met us with her carriage, and drove us to her house at Payhembury. Here we met Miss Hennell and Miss Seton, two young ladies, both daughters of Colonels in the army, who were staying with her, and having put a hamper of provisions into the carriage, we proceeded about two miles to Hembury Fort. The little inn at the foot of the hill is now converted into a farm house, and another has been erected a few yards south. Whilst the ladies were setting out the dinner, Mr. H. and myself took a good ramble beyond the north end, which we had scarcely examined before . . .

We dined on the western agger where there is a seat; and nicely prepared the dinner was! By was of varying the entertainment, Mr. Heineken put on a false nose, unobserved, and opened a large antique clasp knife; and I put on a false nose and a pair of large goggle-eyed spectacles, and pulled the rim of my felt hat over my eyes, and drawing a Chinese dagger cut up my bread and cheese with it, much to the amusement of the ladies, and the astonishment of the boy who attended on us.

(From the Diary)

A Royal Occasion with a Difference

23 May 1881:—

This morning Prince Alfred, Duke of Edinburgh, landed here from the 'Lively' to inspect the Coast Guard. His wife, the sister of the present Emperor of Russia, accompanied him, with Lady Harriet Grimstone and Lieut. Ricard R.N. As there were some waves on the beach, the Life Boat went off, Mr. Floyd, the secretary going too. The Royal Party got into the Life Boat. Mr. Floyd sat on the gunnel, to make more room, and somehow fell overboard. One of the crew named Conant, jumped over after him, and then another called Bartlett; and they soon fished him up. On landing they went to the preventative station at the east end of the beach, where Dr. Pullin of Sidmouth, who holds the appointment of Medical Attendant to the station, gave his Royal Highness a photograph of Woolbrook Glen, at the west end of the beach, where the Queen, as an infant was nursed and where the Duke of Kent died on 23rd January 1820.

The crowd was so great there was no moving. The Duke however, inspected the men and visited their residences. Mrs. Davidson, of Richmond Lodge lent her carriage to go to Exmouth in, and Mr. Chamberlain, of the York Hotel, supplied four horses. The weather was bright and beautiful and they drove over Peak Hill. Mr. Harris the Dairyman, of Sidmouth, also gave them a cream cheese, of all things in the world. On driving into Exmouth the postillions by some awkwardness ran the pole of the carriage into an omnibus and broke it, and the Royal Party were obliged to dismount. There have been many curious stories in circulation about Mr. Floyd's mishap, the cheese, and this event; but as it is hard to get at the true particulars, I let them go. For the last two or three months Mr. Floyd has been far from well, and had been more or less keeping house; and he has told me since that he was not fit to go, and that he supposes he must have fainted, as he lost consciousness. He was only sensible of a rather pleasant sound of water in his ears, and was unable to make any effort to save himself. He would soon have ceased to live if he had not been picked up.

18 Jun:—

The Duke and Duchess of Edinburgh have very kindly sent their photographs down to Mr. Floyd. I have been looking at them today. They are three-quarter figures, and the photos are some seven inches high. The Duke has written his name 'Alfred' at the foot of his portrait and the Duchess has written 'Marie' at the foot of hers.

(Newspaper cutting in Diary)

Cheese presented by Miss Eliza Harris, daughter of the Dairyman Harris: order for more given).

(From the Diary)

Porcine Finale

8 Sept. 1894:—

A concrete wall near the Gas house fell out upon a pigs' shed in which were 15 pigs belonging to Mr. Holmes, my butcher. Two were crushed so that they had to be killed and 13 were smothered and suffocated under the debris of the wall and the shed. MEM:- Don't order any pig for a month.

(Final entry in the Diary).

Undated note on how to help your Executor

A person may with advantage some times be his own Executor, at all events to a certain degree. He who is solicitous in his later years to set his house in order is likely to be predisposed in that direction. What a man can do whilst he is alive, will relieve his Executor from doing it after he is dead. My small oak book case, the carving of which gave me much amusement for considerable time, and which contains a collection of books almost all relating to Sidmouth, together with its stand, is given in my Will to the use of the Free Library at Exeter Museum; but I have decided to send it to them during my life, and this step will save others the trouble of doing it.—P.O.H.

(Undated note at the end of Diary)

Miss Maria Gibbons calls on Peter Orlando Hutchinson

25. Apr. 1887:—

We again started about 9.30 a.m. 'Xenophon Edward' and 'Nem Con' (the donkeys) in splendid condition, 'Romulus' (the black retriever dog) and the writer in high spirits.

At East Budleigh we stopped to pick up the same friend who had joined us on our pleasant Branscombe trip, and then after the short delay of packing the carriage etc, we went gaily on our road to Sidmouth . . . Otterton has much of interest attached to it; indeed in early days the Manor of Sidmouth was only an appendage to that of Otterton, which belonged to the Countess Ghida, the mother of Harold, who fell at the battle of Hastings. William the Conqueror made over Otterton, Sidmouth and other contiguous places to St. Michael's Mount in Normandy . . .

Having thoroughly enjoyed the view from the top of Peak Hill, and thus having given our steeds a little breathing time, we commenced the exceedingly steep descent into Sidmouth. 'Xenophon' and 'Nem Con' have often gone down that hill, but they never got over their dislike for it. However, we found ourselves down in the town, through the whole of which we were obliged to drive as the lodgings we had heard of were in what is called the 'Land Part'.

(Finding Mr. Hutchinson out after arriving at The Old Chancel, with a letter of introduction from a kind friend they visited the church, copied memorials and then . . .)

Proceeded again to the Old Chancel, and were hospitably received; and after being greatly refreshed by some tea, the kindly host showed us some of the unique treasures of his house, beginning at the exquisitely carved and painted ceiling of the room in which we were sitting, in each of the panels of which are the arms of the various lords of the manor, commencing with those of Ghida, mother of Harold. The carving in that and other parts of the house is exquisite, and is the handiwork of the master of the house himself.

Having surveyed the valuable manuscripts and other treasures in this wonderful mansion, we bade farewell to our kindly host and walked to the Glen, where the Duke of Kent died, and where Our Gracious Queen was brought to reside at seven months old.

(From *We Donkeys on the Coast of Devon* Chapter III Outings IV and V).

HUTCHINSON PEDIGREE

Thomas Hutchinson = Margaret Sanford
Governor of Mass. M. 1734
1711-1780 D. 1753

Thomas II = Sarah Oliver
Probate Judge 1745-1802
in Mass.
1740-1811

many offspring

Thomas III 1772-1837
Mary = Oliver 1773-1833
Andrew = Anne Parker 1776-1846
William = Louisa Parker 1778-1816

Young Bingham 1806-1870
Augusta Kingdon
Elizabeth 1808-1809
Louisa 1809-1810
Peter Orlando 1810-1897
Frances Harriet b. 1812 = 1) Rumley 2) Robertson
William George 1813-1822

Augusta Bingham b. 1855
Parker Oliver b. 1857
Mary Kingdon 1859-1864
Orlando Bingham b. 1862
Jane Collingwood b. 1867

(From *Diary & Letters of Thomas Hutchinson* by P.O.H.: Vol. 2, p. 446: and pp. 473 *et seq*.

TITLE PAGE OF DIARY AND LETTERS OF THOMAS HUTCHINSON
by PETER ORLANDO HUTCHINSON

THE
DIARY AND LETTERS
of
HIS EXCELLENCY
THOMAS HUTCHINSON, ESQ.,
B.A., (Harvard) LLD (Oxon)

Captain-General and Governor-in-Chief of
His late Majesty's Province of Massachusetts Bay,
in North America;

With an account of his Administration when he was Member and
Speaker of the House of Representatives, and his Government
of the Colony during the difficult period
that preceded the War of Independence

COMPILED FROM THE ORIGINAL DOCUMENTS STILL REMAINING IN
THE POSSESSION OF HIS DESCENDANTS
BY
PETER ORLANDO HUTCHINSON
one of his great grandsons
Motto for title page of a History of the Revolt of
the Colonies:-
'I have nourished children and brought them up,
and even they have revolted from me'—Isaiah,
I Chap., 2nd Verse. Bp. of London's Translation
(written on fly-leaf of Diary)

BOSTON:
HOUGHTON, MIFFLIN & CO., 4 PARK STREET

1884

(Vol. II was published 1886)

TRANSACTIONS of the DEVONSHIRE ASSOCIATION
ARTICLES contributed by PETER ORLANDO HUTCHINSON

1. On Hill Fortresses, Sling Stones, and other Antiquities in South Eastern Devon. 1868
2. Fossil Elephant's Tooth. 1869
3. On a Second Fossil Tooth found at Sidmouth. 1871
4. Bronze Celt found near Sidmouth. 1872
5. Iron Pits. 1872
6. Fossil Teeth at Sidmouth. 1872
7. Submerged Forest and Mammoth Teeth at Sidmouth. 1873
8. The Population of Sidmouth from 1260 to the present time. 1875
9. Jar found at Musbury. 1876
10. A Scheme for a History of Devonshire. 1877
11. Fossil Plant discovered near Sidmouth. 1879
12. The Site of Moridunum. 1882
13. Honeyditches. 1885

(From obituary notice for Peter Orlando Hutchinson in Transactions 1898, p. 45).

(For other publications and manuscripts see Will p. 120).

This is the last Will and Testament of me Peter Orlando Hutchinson

Of Sidmouth in the County of Devon son of Andrew Hutchinson M.D. Member of the Royal College of Physicians F.R.S. and his wife Anne (married at Kingston-on-Thames in 1805) daughter of Vice Admiral Sir William Parker of Harburn Co. Warwick Bart. and his wife Jane Collingwood And whereas my Brother Young Bingham Hutchinson married Augusta Kingdon of Heavitree near Exeter in 1852 and settled on his own land in Hindmarsh Valley in South Australia and dying in 1870 left a widow and four surviving children namely Augusta Bingham born in 1855: Parker Oliver born in 1857: Orlando Bingham in 1862. and Jane Collingwood born in 1867 who are still living And whereas my sister Frances Harriet married Captain Charles Rumley eldest son of Genl Rumley of Arcot House Sidmouth and settled on their own estate in South Australia and secondly she married Mr. John Robertson of Strowan Grove near Salisbury in the same colony and she became a widow for the second time in 1870 having had no issue All the particulars concerning my family and relatives are fully given in the Pedigree at the end of the second Volume of the *Diary and Letters of Thomas Hutchinson late Governor of Massachusetts Bay in North America* recently published by me Whereas I stand possessed of the freehold of No. 4 Coburg Terrace Sidmouth in the County of Devon which my late father bought of Sir John Kennaway of Escot Bart together with the gravel road and iron boundary railings in front and the yard and premises out to the lane at the back And whereas I purchased of Sir John

Kennaway a long piece of field running about 450 feet more or less in a northerly direction to the garden wall of Blackmore Hall and Grinfield otherwise Hillsdon House the public having a right of way to and from the church at that end including the hedge on the west side and the iron fences on the other sides which I had made and paid for and I afterwards built thereon a stone dwelling in the Gothic style commonly called The Old Chancel the Chapel-like building on the east of the entrance Hall having been made out of material from the Chancel of the Parish Church at the time when the church was rebuilt in 1860 and the grounds and premises of these two tenements adjoin one another And whereas my late Mother received nearly £11,000 from her parents Sir William and Lady Parker of which I had my share and with part of which I bought Preference stock in the Great Western Railway and I am now registered in the Books of the stocks of the company as the proprietor of 360 shares of their Consolidated 4 per centum Irredeemable Preference stock representing a capital of £3000 the certificate of which numbered 1792 and bearing date May 17 1878 is in my cast iron chest painted green with my title deeds and some other things Wherefore I give and bequeath my said railway stock to my Executors or acting Executor In trust to receive the dividends and interest on it and to employ the said interest as I now direct namely To pay the sum of Twenty-eight (£28) free of duty every year to my servant Ann Carslake Newton which I now bequeath to her as an annuity for and during the whole term of her natural life she having lived in my service since January 1869 to be paid to her in four quarterly payments of seven pounds each at the usual quarter days the first payment of seven pounds I request to be made if possible on the first quarter day after my death and the last payment of seven pounds to be made on the quarter day next before or preceeding her death and for their trouble in so doing four times a year I give to them or him the sum of ten shillings as often as the sum of seven pounds is so paid to my servant And after the death of the said annuitant Ann Carslake Newton and after all my debts and legacies shall have been paid and my Executors and Executor secured from any pecuniary loss on my account I give and bequeath the said railway stock to my said sister Frances Harriet Robertson for her sole and separate use but if she be dead I desire that the same be divided equally among the surviving children of my said late brother Whereas when the colony of South Australia was founded in or about the year 1836 my late father gave one hundred pounds (£100) for section 18 of 134 acres of land lying on the west side of the mouth of the river Hindmarsh at Port Victor and whereas in 1876 I sold the same for the sum of one thousand pounds (£1000) with which money I subsequently purchased the ten bonds of £100 each at 96⅜ of the South Australian Loan of January 1. 1876 at 4 per centum per annum and which bonds I have deposited together with the coupons belonging to them at the Devon and Cornwall Bank in the Cathedral Yard in the City of Exeter in England the same yielding me £40 per annum Wherefore I now give and bequeath the said bonds of £100 each together with the remainder of the coupons belonging to them to my acting Executors or

Executor in trust to employ the interest thereof in the execution of the trust imposed upon him or them in this my Will if the same is not sufficiently provided for above and when all debts and legacies and expenses are fully paid and satisfied I give and bequeath the bonds of £100 each together with the coupons belonging to them to my nephew Peter Oliver Hutchinson and to his heirs absolutely and if he is dead I give the same to his executors or administrators for the benefit of his estate And whereas I have already in my lifetime given my various articles of silver plate and jewellery with other things which need not be enumerated and a selection of my books and papers to the children of my late brother who are in South Australia as mentioned above although all the said goods and chattels may not yet have been sent out to them and as to the Hutchinson Papers so called which I sold to the Trustees of the British Museum for the sum of £100 and from which I compiled the Diary and Letters of Thomas Hutchinson late Governor of Massachusetts Bay in two volumes I stand possessed of the copyright that work Wherefore I now give and bequeath the said copyright with all its privileges and emoluments to my cousin Sanford William Hutchinson I give and bequeath free of duty to the Mayor Alderman and Burgesses of the City of Exeter for the use of the Albert Memorial Museum and Free Library in Queen Street my small oak bookcase together with the stand on which it is placed designed in Tudor Gothic which I have myself recently carved for the purpose of holding a collection of books mostly relating to Sidmouth the following being a List of those that at present are contained in it namely:

A collection of Sidmouth Guides from the first in 1810 to the present time as local literature.
My Diary from 1848 to the present time referring to events in Sidmouth
The Diary and Letters of Thomas Hutchinson late Governor of Massechusetts in North America in 2 vols edited by me
Contents of the Sidmouth Parish Chest in MS
Collection of my articles on local antiquities with the illustrations
Dialogues of the Statues extracted from the late Metropolitan Magazine
My MS History of Sidmouth in 5 volumes 4to and bound in green vellum
Rev E Butcher's Excursion from Sidmouth to Chester and back Frontispiece 1806
The Charities of Sidmouth compiled (by me) from the documents in the possession of the Feofees 1867
The Geology of Sidmouth (by me) a juvenile performance 1843
The Restoration or rather Rebuilding of Sidmouth Church (by me) with illustrations &c 1860
The Ferns of Sidmouth (by me) with 20 illustrations 1862
The Flowering Plants and Ferns of Sidmouth and its vicinity by Rev. Rd. Cresswell Curate of Salcombe Regis 1846
Abstract of the Title of the Manor of Sidmouth from 1709 to 1813 Office copy
Volume of cuttings from Newspapers, Magazines, &c.

Volume of impressions of engravings on copper, steel, wood, etc.
Memoirs of John Rattenbury the smuggler portrait printed at Sidmouth 1837
Rifled shot in smoothbore guns Pamphlet 1860
Bye Laws of the Local Board of Sidmouth 1864
Map of the Parish of Sidmouth reduced (by me) from the large map in the possession of the lord of the Manor
Two large folio volumes written by me being the MS from which the vols. of the Diary and Letters of Thomas Hutchinson as above were printed
I give the above enumerated books free of duty and also the following if I do not give them during my life namely—
Observations upon Caesar's Commentaries Long folio curious plates by Clement Edmunds 1665
The Navigations of Nicholas Nicholay Daulphinois Lord of Arfeuile &c &c as to Soliman Emperor of the Turks 1685
The Travels of Busbequius Ambassador to Sultan Soliman temp. Eliz. edition of 1761
Pomponii Melos De Situ Orbis 1787 with numerous old maps mostly dedicated to Devonshire families
Also I give five pounds (£5) free of duty to the use of the Exeter Museum and Free Library

I give and bequeath to the Devon and Exeter Hospital in the County of the City of Exeter to its use and benefit and free of duty the sum of five pounds (£5) my late father having been one of the physicians there I give and bequeath the sum of ten pounds (£10) free of duty to Mrs. Leah Knowles widow of East Budleigh near Sidmouth sister to my servant Ann Carslake Newton and now also in my service And whereas one of my intended Executors has been unexpectedly removed by death wherefore having every confidence in the integrity and intelligence of my cousin Sanford William Hutchinson clerk in Holy Orders I appoint him sole Trustee and Executor to this my Will and I give and bequeath to him the sum of twenty pounds (£20) over and above any other bequest or bequests I may herein make in his favour And as to my said two houses of messuages with their premises and land the one being 4 Coburg Terrace Sidmouth as already described and the other being The Old Chancel with its premises and field as also described above I give devise and bequeath the same to my said cousin and Executor and to his heirs only on the condition now to be named that is to say if and on condition that he do pay or cause to be paid within twelve months after my death and free of duty or unnecessary deductions the clear sum of four hundred pounds (£400) to the surviving children of my said late brother which they can divide among themselves But if it should so happen that my said cousin and Executor should not be so disposed as to accept the condition and pay the sum named I then request that within the space of one year after my death he do offer for sale either by public auction or private contract both my houses together with their premises and land in one lot for as the houses are so close together it will be apparent to the owner of The Old Chancel and he will see the advisability of retaining some authority over the occupier of the other and this point should be made plain to any intending purchaser And as to the proceeds and profits accruing from such sale and after all expenses attending this division of my affairs are paid and fully satisfied I will that the remainder of the money be given to the surviving children of my above said late brother share and share alike And after the houses have thus been disposed of it is my will that a sale may be affected of the furniture and effects belonging to me that may be in either or both of the said houses except the following articles which I give and bequeath to my said cousin and Executor Sanford William Hutchinson that is to say Being at the present time kept in that part of the building especially called The Old Chancel I give him the papers books and other effects and the old Oak chest in which they are kept Also the cast iron chest painted green and the deeds and papers commonly kept in it Also the weapons and sticks on the mantel shelf Also all fossils antiques and cabinets with all boxes and their contents in any part of the house where I live Also the Crown Derby Spode and all the best china and glass that ought not to be sold together with all my books pictures drawings and engravings and all linen cotton and woollen articles and all other goods chattels and effects not coming under the common denomination of furniture and my wearing apparel may be dealt with as he pleases My silver plate I have not mentioned in this my Will because I have already given it and set it aside for my late brother's children And as to the residue of my estate and effects whatsoever and wheresoever in England or in Australia or anywhere else and of what kind so ever the same may be I give devise and bequeath the same to my nephew Parker Oliver Hutchinson and to his heirs And I now revoke cancel and annul all former Wills and Codicils dated this eleventh day of September One thousand eight hundred and ninety four

Peter Orlando Hutchinson

Signed by the said Peter Orlando Hutchinson the Testator as his last Will and Testament in the presence of us being present at the same time who at his request in his presence and in the presence of each other subscribe our names as witnesses

John William Barrow Clerk in Holy Orders

H. S. J. Edmonson Wrenford Sidford Sidmouth Clerk in Holy Orders

On the 8th day of November 1897 Probate of this Will was granted to the Reverend Sanford William Hutchinson Clerk the sole Executor (of Blurton Vicarage Stoke-on-Trent Staffordshire)

Personal estate 8th November 1897

Gross	£5,631.13/2
Net	£5,255.7/7